EATING ANIMALS

also by elizabeth minchilli

Italian Rustic

Private Tuscany

Villas on the Italian Lakes

Restoring a Home in Italy

Private Rome

Deruta

elizabeth minchilli

EATING ROME

living the good life
in the eternal city

St. Martin's Griffin ✖ New York

www.stmartins.com

Endpaper and text photographs courtesy of the author

Designed by Ralph Fowler / rlfdesign
Production manager: Adriana Coada

The Library of Congress Cataloging-in-Publication Data is available upon request.

ISBN 978-1-250-04768-7 (trade paperback)
ISBN 978-1-250-04784-7 (e-book)

St. Martin's Griffin books may be purchased for educational, business, or promotional use. For information on bulk purchases, please contact the Macmillan Corporate and Premium Sales Department at 1-800-221-7945, extension 5442, or write to specialmarkets@macmillan.com.

First Edition: April 2015

10 9 8 7 6 5 4 3 2 1

For Sophie and Emma, my Roman daughters

contents

acknowledgments

It is hard to thank an entire city, but I would like to say *mille grazie* to the men and women who own and work in the restaurants, bars, markets, *gelaterie,* bakeries, and other places that feed my family in Rome on a daily basis and who have taught me so much.

While I love the world of social media, and have many virtual friends out there who inspire and encourage me daily, I also have close friends here in Rome who have been my partners in crime as I try out new restaurants, test new cocktails, and generally use them as guinea pigs for recipes. Thank you, Jane Wietsma Gudgeon and Gillian Longworth McGuire. I know you've often sacrificed your slim figures for my benefit, and I thank you.

An extra-special thanks to author, chef, radio host extraordinaire, and "sister" Evan Kleiman, whom I have been cooking, eating, and traveling with for almost two decades. You have taught me more than you know.

Without my blog, this book would not have happened. And without my loyal readers, the blog would not exist. So mega thanks to all of you for being so supportive from the very beginning. While it may be my life here in Rome that I'm writing about, it is your comments, suggestions, and kind words that not only keep it going, but keep it growing.

One reader gets an extra-special mention: my editor at St. Martin's, Michael Flamini. Thank you, Michael, not only for being a loyal fan but for having the fantastic idea of turning my blog into this book. You are the best!

Working with St. Martin's has been a dream. Rarely have I felt so loved and appreciated while working on a project. Thank you to everyone, especially Olga Grlic for the beautiful cover design. Vicki Lame wrangled my disparate mix of chapters, lists, photographs, and bits and pieces, and she managed to log them in and pass them along to the powers that be. The beautiful interior design is thanks to James Sinclair and Ralph Fowler. Additional thanks to Adriana Coada, Emily Walters, Kathryn Hough, Karlyn Hixson, Laura Clark, and the rest of the St. Martin's Press team.

Thank you to my agent, Elizabeth Kaplan, whose balance of sane advice and boundless enthusiasm is just what I need.

As ever, my family gets the biggest thanks of all. First and foremost to my parents, Joseph Helman and Barbara Wood. How on earth you had the courage to pick up your three children and move halfway across the world to Rome, I'll never understand. But I am very glad you did. Thanks to my "other" parents, Ursula Helman and Roger Wood, for their love and support. And to my sisters, Robin Helman Whitney and Jodi Helman Multer: I'm glad you were part of this delicious adventure from the very beginning. Although most people complain about their mothers-in-law, mine has not only been an inspiration, but has generously passed along her knowledge, from her kitchen to mine. Thank you, Rosa.

Finally to Domenico, Sophie, and Emma. You are the main subject of my blog, my book, and my life. I'm not sure you signed up for this, but I hope you're enjoying it as much as I am. *Mille baci.*

EATING ROME

the city that feeds me

When I was twelve years old, I decided I wanted to go away to camp. I'm not quite sure where this desire came from, since I was far from sporty. I was definitely the one who was picked last for soccer and the entire idea of dodgeball still gives me nightmares. So it couldn't have been the lure of water-skiing or canoeing that made me think I'd like to spend two months by a cold lake in Wisconsin. I think I must have been more attracted to the idea of s'mores by the campfire and perfecting the baked beans I had learned how to make at a Girl Scout cookout.

Once I got to camp I soon realized my mistake. After failing to ever stand up on my water skis and downright refusing to go for any frigid 6:00 a.m. wake-up swims, I tried to stay in the craft house, working on my ceramic and weaving skills while counting the days until I could finally return home and get back to the life I knew and loved in St. Louis.

While I was away at camp my parents decided to go on their version of camp as well. A three-week trip to Europe for the first time took them to Venice, Florence, and Rome. It was 1972 and Italy must have appeared to be almost like a different planet from suburban St. Louis. The language, the food, the life was like nothing they had ever seen. Rather than take home simple souvenirs of their time in Italy, they took home a plan, which they shared with me on my first day back at home from camp.

As I was happily unpacking my trunk, my mother came in to tell me that I'd soon be packing it again. "We're moving to Italy," she said. My father had sold his business, an art gallery, to our next-door neighbor, and the house where I had grown up was already rented to another family. They were arriving on September 1. And we were leaving.

How they had the courage to pick up three young children and move to a country where they didn't speak the language and knew no one is beyond me. I am pretty sure my grandparents thought they were insane. I know I did.

I was aghast. My school, my friends, my Barbies! Everything that I knew, and that I had desperately missed over the two months spent at camp, was being ripped away from me. But as I dried my tears and packed my Barbies (there was at least that small comfort) I got ready for what was to be one of the most important events in my life.

While there were the usual hiccups of moving to any new city—missing the school bus on the first day; making new friends—I soon shed the fears and misgivings that any twelve-year-old would have, and traded them in for a head-over-heels, lifelong love affair with this ancient city. Although we only spent two years living in Rome, they were impressionable ones. Many of the strongest memories I have from my child-hood date from this time, and—not surprisingly—most of them have to do with food. The discovery of *pizza bianca*, hot from the corner bakery; the sharp smell of piles of artichokes in the open market; a cone filled with melon *gelato* that was like biting into the sweetest, juiciest piece of fruit I'd ever had. Food has been one of the most impor-tant things in my life for as long as I can re-member. And my relationship with eating, cooking, shopping, and feeding my family is intricately tied to the rhythms and tradi-tions of this ancient city.

I came back to Rome—and to Europe and Italy—as often as I could over the following years, not only for vacations during the summers with my family but also for sev-eral semesters abroad in France, Germany, Spain, and Italy while studying French, German, Spanish, and Italian.

Eventually, I moved here on my own. In graduate school I chose my topic well: Sixteenth-century garden architecture would essentially guarantee that I would spend at least two years in Italy. I applied for and received a grant that allowed me to read my way through Medici documents in the archives in Florence. My mornings were spent sorting through ancient shop-ping lists and architectural sketches in a back room at the Uffizi. Afternoons were spent not only writing but also shopping, cooking, and wandering through the cob-blestoned streets of Florence and the sur-rounding Tuscan countryside.

After two perfect years, my time in Flor-ence ran out. I had finished my research and now had to face the facts (a) I had to actually write the dissertation, (b) I had to move back to the United States, and (c) if everything went according to plan I would hopefully get a job teaching art history at some university far from where I really wanted to be: Italy.

So I was already rethinking my commitment to academia when the inevitable happened. I met and fell in love with the Italian man of my dreams: Domenico. I left Florence and settled down permanently in the city I had always truly considered home in my heart: Rome.

In very quick succession, I found myself with an Italian husband, an Italian dog, an Italian home, an Italian baby, and a brand-new job in Italy. A friend had recently launched an art newspaper in New York and asked me to begin contributing features for the magazine section. I figured that since I was just sitting around being pregnant, why not?

After four of my features appeared on the cover, a check arrived in the mail. My shock was considerable. After eight years of graduate school, I didn't realize that you could write about art and actually get paid to do so. I could do this for a living!

I soon expanded my coverage to include interior design and architecture as well as travel, food, gardens, and just about any other lifestyle topic that came my way, for publications such as *Architectural Digest, Bon Appétit, Food & Wine, Town & Country,* and *The Financial Times.* At the same time, I began writing big, fancy coffee-table books about beautiful things like Tuscan villas, Umbrian castles, and handmade ceramics.

It was when it came time to publicize my last book, *Italian Rustic,* that my publisher suggested the trifecta of Facebook, Twitter, and blogging. After a life spent writing away in the solitude of my own little garret in Rome, I found the wide world of social media exciting and inspiring. Although I had been writing all of my life, I had never had direct contact with my audience.

At the beginning I had a hard time wrapping my head around what I wanted to say on my blog. Coming from a professional world of detailed assignments, it was difficult to know exactly how to frame it. So, rather than make any decision, I just decided to record what I was up to, day by day.

As it turns out, most of what I do, every single day, has a lot to do with food, and since I am living in Rome, the city provided a framework. So while I never planned to write a food blog from this ancient city, that is exactly what it turned out to be. My blog, *Elizabeth Minchilli in Rome,* lets me share what I love best—eating, traveling, cooking, and all sorts of other good stuff. My *Eat Italy* apps, *Eat Rome, Eat Florence,* and *Eat Venice,* are guides to my favorite restaurants, coffee bars, markets, and gelaterie in those cities.

Eating Rome is my homage to the city that feeds me—literally and figuratively. It is a personal, quirky, and (I hope) fun look at the city through my own food-focused vision. This is how I experience Rome, day by day, bite by bite.

a sweet start to every roman day

Breakfast is still something I have issues with in Italy. While I embrace all other meal-times with open arms, and traditional Italian recipes fill not only my blog but my life, Italian breakfast has made almost no appearance. And when you think about it, I'm not alone. While there are cookbooks out for everything from Italian market cooking to Italian baking, I don't think I've ever seen anything giving culinary advice about Italian breakfasts.

That is for a very good reason. Italian breakfasts are nonevents. Whoever decided that breakfast is the most important meal of the day was certainly not speaking in Italian.

If you ask most Italians what they have for breakfast many will respond, *"Non mangio niente"* ("I don't eat anything"). A quick espresso—either at home or at a bar—will do them until lunch. And those who do actually eat something? If they happen by a coffee bar then a *cornetto* (that would be Italian for "croissant") is standard.

At home? It's cake or cookie time.

Even though Domenico has become completely Americanized over the years, when it comes to breakfast he is pure Italian. There's nothing he likes better than a handful of cookies he can dip into his *caffèlatte* while he reads the paper. Yes, Italians eat cookies for breakfast. While in the States you have entire supermarket aisles dedicated to cereal, in

Italy you can walk down breakfast cookie lane.

While these packaged biscuits are a relatively modern development, having a slice of cake in the morning is something that is more rustic and traditional. In fact, when Domenico and I first started dating in Florence, I am pretty sure he ended up marrying me because I served him a corn flour breakfast cake, *amor polenta*, for breakfast. I think I bought it because the recipe had the word *amor* in it, and I thought it would make him "amor" me all the more. It did.

For about the last ten years there has been a new trend in Roman restaurants to serve brunch. When I first starting reading about this new phenomenon I was thrilled. Finally, I thought, we can go out to a restaurant and get eggs, pancakes, and, hope beyond hope, even bagels.

I should have known better. When Italians co-opt American food phrases they often get them slightly wrong. In this case, in Rome, when someone (and by someone I mean a trendy restaurant) says brunch, what they really mean is an all-you-can-eat Sunday buffet at a fixed price that starts at noon and goes on until about 3:00 p.m. But at least in my informal survey of the most popular brunches around, no identifiable breakfast foods make any appearance whatsoever.

In our own home, I've tried over the years to dedicate Sundays to preparing a traditional American breakfast. And if Sophie is a big fan of anything to do with pork, Emma has the sweet tooth in our family, and truly American Sunday breakfasts are one of her favorite meals. Pancakes, of course, are easy since flour and eggs are pretty universal ingredients. Maple syrup? Not so much, so cherry preserves usually play that role. Bacon and eggs similarly become pancetta and eggs, which is all right with me.

And then there are times when I just give in and decide that a sweet and fluffy treat is OK for breakfast. That's when I head out to my local coffee bar for breakfast. This was definitely something that took some getting used to. I'm a slow riser, and lingering over a mug of coffee and eventually moving on to breakfast while reading the news is my idea of an acceptable start to the day. The Roman ritual of stopping by the local bar takes a whole other level of early morning social skills.

Every Roman has a favorite coffee bar. This is a very important point to make and involves several deciding factors. First and foremost is location. Italians are creatures of habit, and so the bar where you stop for your first coffee of the morning has to be on your morning route, not only for convenience but also from a social point of view.

On your way to work, you may decide to stop at the bar below your home, or one nearer to your office. It could depend on the quality of the coffee, but more likely it has something to do with your desire to chat with people from your neighborhood, or people from work. Or maybe you meet other parents for a quick coffee after dropping the kids off at school. The point is, since the timing is the same every day, you don't really have to make plans to meet up with people, it just naturally happens.

And then there is the interaction with the owners of the bar. I find it pretty amazing how much I know about the personal life of the guy who has been pulling my espresso for the last fifteen years.

Once you've ordered your coffee (and see chapter 6 for that) it's time to decide what to eat. And this is where choosing your breakfast locale correctly becomes essential. Not all cornetti are created equal. And certainly not all bars bake their own.

The Holy Grail in terms of breakfast bars is to find one that is also a *pasticceria*, or "pastry shop." There are some bars that make excellent coffee, and then there are pastry shops that bake fresh pastries—including cornetti—on the premises, every day. Most bars, while serving cornetti, buy them from a bakery. A recent trend for some bars is to buy frozen, unbaked cornetti, and bake them on the premises. It's not a bad alternative. And some bars do indeed get superb cornetti brought in daily.

But much better to go to a place that does this sort of thing professionally—makes both pastries and coffee. You would think that this kind of combination would be easy to find, but instead it's a dying breed that survives, for the most part, in the areas of Rome that are heavily residential, and in neighborhoods that I, and probably you, wouldn't necessarily go to. They are the types of places I always hear people talk about, but somehow never make it to.

One I had heard about for ages is the Pasticceria Siciliana Svizzera. I'd always been fascinated by the name. Friends talk about it, in loving terms, as one of those Roman classics. When I ask, "What do you mean? Switzerland and Sicily? What's that about?" they just kind of give me a blank stare. Like, duh, of course there is a pastry shop in Rome that combines traditions from southern Italy with those north of the Alps.

It has always remained a bit of a mystery to me due partly to its location. It's along the Via Gregorio VII, in a weird piazza that's not really a piazza, Pio XI. I'd seen it many times, as we were heading toward the Aurelia, on our way out of town. But if you know Rome, and you've ever driven on Via Gregorio VII, then you will understand why I couldn't simply pull over. Gregorio VII is one of the most frustrating streets in Rome: stoplights where you don't expect them, seemingly nowhere to turn off, and absolutely no way (that I can see) of making a U-turn once you've driven past a delicious-looking pastry shop. In other words, a typical Roman street.

But recently I had to take our car in for its annual checkup, which is something my daughter usually does and why I never realized the garage is located in Piazza Pio XI! Once I got the car all settled in for its overnight visit, I took my life in my hands, crossed the "piazza," dodging drivers who were obviously as confused as I always felt, and eventually got through the front doors of the pasticceria.

I finally understood what all the fuss was about: Cases groaning with Sicilian goodies. Baroque *cassate*, with crowns of candied fruit. Mini versions of cassate, *cannoli*, and other almond-based pastries. What was Swiss? I guess it must have been the more ornate cakes, piled high with whipped cream, chocolate, nuts, and berries. They certainly didn't look Italian to me, and since I don't quite know what Swiss cakes look like, they convinced me.

It turns out I was right. According to their website, in the nineteenth century a few famous Swiss pastry makers moved to southern Italy—to Palermo, Naples, and Catania. The result was a marriage between the Arab-influenced Sicilian tradition and the more refined Swiss. And so the southern Italian repertoire was enriched by about a hundred recipes using things like whipped cream, chocolate, and pastry cream. In other words: fancy cakes.

Since it was 9:00 a.m., I thought it best to skip the whipped cream and chocolate and, instead, went straight for the morning pastry section, which all the obviously regular locals were doing already. Although the doughnuts and brioche looked tempting, I fell for the cream- and raisin-studded Danish. And don't think I'm just calling it a Danish because I'm American. They actually call them *Danese*. So there.

Another pastry shop that I don't get to as often as I should is Natalizi. Again, this treasure is located in a neighborhood—on the border of Parioli—that usually lacks any reason to go to. But on my yearly visit to my accountant I make the effort to get there by breakfast time, before they run out of cream-filled *maritozzi*, egg-glazed yeast buns.

I actually hadn't been to Natalizi in a few years and was a bit scared it might not be there anymore. Thankfully, nothing had changed at all. It is one of Rome's oldest pastry shops and its kitchens below the shop take care of catering some of Rome's fanciest parties in private villas. The glass display case still stretched along one side of the small store, filled with old-fashioned éclairs, cream-filled puff pastries, and my personal favorite: a sugar-encrusted, whipped cream–filled choux pastry. I paid the cashier, picked up my pastry, and wiggled myself a space standing at the curved bar between neighborhood regulars. An espresso certainly woke me up on that rainy morning, and the sweet treat definitely gave me strength for my visit to the accountant. (I'm shallow that way.)

my favorite places for a sweet breakfast in rome

Natalizi

Via Po 124, 39-06-8535-0736
➤ An old-fashioned pastry shop and coffee bar, located near the Parioli neighborhood.

Vanni

Via Col di Lana 10, 39-06-3254-9012

➤ This is a Roman institution, and serves everything from breakfast to dinner. The pastries are all made on the premises, and there's nothing better than one of their cream-filled cornetti and a cappuccino.

Pasticceria Siciliana Svizzera

Piazza Pio XI 10, 39-06-637-4974

➤ A place that is well known by most Romans, but located in a very residential neighborhood up behind the Vatican. A great place to stop on your way out of town, on the Aurelia, to the beach.

Panella

Via Merulana 54, 39-06-487-2435

➤ Panella has long been known as one of the best bakeries in town, and they have recently expanded to include a coffee bar as well.

Dagnino

Via Emanuele Orlando 75, 39-06-481-8660

➤ Sicilian specialties in a strange 1970s shopping arcade not far from Piazza Repubblica.

Lotti

Via Sardegna 13/21, 39-06-482-1902

➤ It's not easy to find something cozy and comfortable near superfancy Via Veneto. This place makes all their own pastries, and has both outdoor and indoor tables where you can enjoy breakfast.

recipes

ciambella

Makes one 10-inch cake

This is about as simple and straight-forward a breakfast cake as you can get. *Ciambella* sort of translates as "donut," but it refers to the shape—round with a hole in the middle—and not the pastry. It's basically a pound cake, but made in a tube pan. It's perfect in the morning since it's not too, too sweet, and a slice dunked in a big cup of *caffèlatte* is just right.

> Butter and bread crumbs, for the
>   baking pan
> 3 large eggs
> 1½ cups (340 grams) sugar
> 1 teaspoon pure vanilla extract
> 2½ cups (275 grams) all-purpose flour
> 2 teaspoons baking powder
> 1 teaspoon salt
> 1½ cups (350 milliliters) heavy cream

Preheat the oven to 350°F (180°C). Butter a 10-inch tube pan, and coat with bread crumbs

In a small bowl, beat the eggs and sugar until light yellow and fluffy. Add the vanilla and mix to incorporate. In a separate large bowl, mix the baking powder and salt into flour.

Add the flour and cream to the egg-sugar mixture, alternating the dry with the

(continued)

wet, until incorporated. Do not overmix. Pour the batter into the prepared pan.

Bake for 40 minutes, or when a knife inserted into the cake comes out clean.

Remove from the oven and let cool for 10 minutes. Invert the pan, gently tapping on it, until the cake slips out. Let cool on a rack and serve.

amor polenta

Serves 8

This is my favorite Italian breakfast cake. It's actually made in a special pan (known as a rehrücken pan) that is curved and ridged. The ridges make it easy to divide the cake into portions. But don't worry if you can't find one (they are even hard to find in Italy); you can make it in a loaf pan and it will be just as delicious.

- 8 tablespoons (1 stick/110 grams) unsalted butter, at room temperature, plus some for the pan
- 2 large eggs
- ½ cup (115 grams) granulated sugar
- 2 teaspoons pure vanilla extract
- ¾ cup (130 grams) finely ground corn flour (I use Mulino Marino's polenta: half fine and half Grusera)
- 1 cup (110 grams) all-purpose flour
- 2 teaspoons baking powder
- 1 cup (170 grams) ground almonds
- Powdered sugar, for dusting

Preheat the oven to 350°F (180°C). Butter the baking pan.

In a large bowl, beat the softened butter, eggs, and granulated sugar until well combined. Add the vanilla.

Add the two flours, baking powder, and almonds and mix to incorporate. Pour the batter into the prepared pan.

Bake for 40 minutes. Remove from the oven and let cool in the pan.

When cool, remove the cake from the pan by inverting it onto a plate, and dust with the powdered sugar.

pisciotta

Serves 6

I'm always amazed that there are still recipes from Marcella Hazan's *The Classic Italian Cookbook* that I haven't cooked yet. I thought that over the last twenty years or so I must have cooked, baked, or fried just about every recipe in her books. But no, I'm always discovering something new. *Pisciotta*. Olive oil cake. Perfect. Except for that name. *Pisciotta*? Really? I'm not sure where Marcella got this name from, but she claimed it was an old recipe from Verona. I did write to her (we were friends on Facebook!) and she wrote back: "*Ciao,* Elizabeth, I should have asked Nori Dalla Rosa, but I didn't. Sometimes one overlooks the most obvious questions. My son teaches in a villa near the trattoria, and if I remember, and he remembers, I'll ask him to inquire, should he drop in for lunch. Or you could

But back to the name of the cake. *Pisciotta*. Marcella sadly passed away before she could get back to me with the answer. But the mystery and the cake—like so many of her recipes—live on.

(Adapted from Marcella Hazan's *Essentials of Classic Italian Cooking*.)

¾ cup fruity extra-virgin olive oil, plus
    more for the pan

2 large eggs

½ cup (115 grams) sugar

⅓ cup (80 milliliters) whole milk

⅓ cup (80 milliliters) dry Marsala wine

1½ cups (165 grams) all-purpose flour

1 tablespoon baking powder

½ teaspoon salt

1 tablespoon ground cinnamon

2 teaspoons ground ginger

Preheat the oven to 350°F (180°C). Grease a 2¼-quart tube pan with a bit of the olive oil.

In a large bowl, beat the eggs and sugar until light and fluffy. Add the milk, Marsala, and the ¾ cup of olive oil and mix well. In a separate bowl, mix together the dry ingredients.

Add the dry ingredients to the egg mixture and stir to combine. Pour the batter into the prepared pan.

Bake in the middle of the oven for about 45 minutes. Remove from the oven and let cool for about 10 minutes.

When cool, loosen the cake from the pan with a knife, invert it onto a plate, then flip it over so the risen side faces up.

phone them. I am glad you are using the cookbook. *Saluti*. Marcella"

If you are from Rome, the word *pisciotta* sounds more like something you'd do into a fountain, if you get my meaning. Sophie decided it referred to the long yellow stream of olive oil as you pour it into the bowl. Whatever.

The one ingredient that Marcella's recipe called for that I didn't have was lemon zest, which I think would have been perfect. Instead I added hefty doses of ground cinnamon and ginger, which were spicy and kind of festive.

shopping in the markets of rome

f there is one quintessential image that people have of food and Italy it has got to be the open-air market. The image probably includes farmers hawking their apples and oranges, fishmongers slapping around sea bass and squid, and butchers hacking off huge *bistecche* to wrap up in a rough piece of brown paper to take home for the family meal.

Unfortunately, these days, you are more likely to enjoy this image at a Fellini revival than in downtown Rome. For better or (usually) for worse, the open-air market that was the mainstay of shopping for hundreds of years has changed drastically and rapidly in the last three decades.

When I first moved to Rome in 1972 the open-air markets were still going strong. In fact, one of my most vivid memories of that period is walking into Campo de' Fiori and being hit by an intense smell that I could not identify. I'd grown up in St. Louis, and while I had always enjoyed trips to Schnucks and Bettendorf's to do the weekly shopping with my mother, I certainly don't associate any specific aroma with that time. Boxed cereal, pints of cottage cheese, and even shiny piles of apples just aren't that aromatic.

But the wall of perfume that hit me as Via dei Giubbonari opened up onto the packed square was intense. Since the butcher stands were on the left side of the square, it was the smell of raw meat that came first. Up until then, our ground hamburger had come neatly shrink-wrapped in little Styrofoam trays, so I don't think I realized raw meat even had a smell. Slightly sweet, and not always entirely appetizing, it was, I think, the first time I truly realized that meat actually comes from animals.

And to the right, the corner near the water fountain was given over to the fish vendors. Selling out early in the morning, the fish on display—*spigole* (sea bass), *orate* (bream), and *triglie* (red mullet)—were sold whole, complete with heads and tails. The process of gutting the fish, which would be done only once they had been sold, produced its own distinctive, acrid smell.

But the one overwhelming olfactory experience for me was only fully explained decades later when I moved back to Rome as a young wife. There was one slightly bitter but fresh and green smell that I would recognize in an instant as the "Campo de' Fiori" smell. But if you had asked me then what exactly it was, I could not have told you. Somehow I thought it was just a generic market smell.

But back at home, thirty years later, unpacking my produce and getting ready to cook lunch for my family, I finally realized that the unique smell that had survived in my Proustian food memory was that of perhaps the most iconic of Roman vegetables: the artichoke. And yes, I know you are probably thinking that artichokes don't have a smell. And if you are buying yours in a supermarket in Des Moines or Chicago,

then they don't. But if you are lucky enough to wander over to one of the massive piles of green and purple globes that fill the markets in Rome during the late spring and early summer, then you'll be enveloped in the essence of spring.

the market today

Campo de' Fiori is a market in Rome that a lot of people love. It is also a market that a lot of people love to hate. The open-air market in Campo de' Fiori is undeniably one of Rome's most famous piazze. Much of this has to do with its location. It is pretty much the only open-air market left in the center of Rome. Each of Rome's *rione,* or "neighborhoods," used to have an open-air market. And when I first moved back to Rome in the early 1990s, I'd do much of my shopping in markets that were steps away from the Trevi Fountain, the Spanish Steps, and the Viminale.

Sadly, things change. Due to transformed shopping habits, rising real estate prices, and shifting family customs, most of these markets have died a slow death over the last two decades.

One of the reasons is the explosion of lower-priced supermarkets that descended on the city. They are obviously cheaper, and often more convenient. Another reason is the changing shopping habits. Wives and *nonne* no longer shop daily for the main meal prepared for husbands and sons who come home from work for lunch. Most women work these days, and so families tend to do their shopping on weekends, at the less expensive supermarkets. And finally, rising real estate prices and taxes have made selling apples and oranges from a cart not so much of a career calling.

Like the other markets in Rome, Campo de' Fiori was dying its own slow death. By the early '90s the market was a far cry from the one I remembered from the time I lived here as a child in the 1970s. The modern version was not the crowded, chaotic, and colorful mash-up of fruits, vegetables, meats, fish, cheeses, and flowers that I loved. When I moved back to Rome in 1990, instead of massive piles of artichokes and melons, there were stretches of empty cobblestoned paving where stands used to crowd one another out. Each year, as I pushed my daughter's stroller around the square, there would be fewer and fewer stands, and more and more empty space. The meat vendors were the first to go, then the fish vendors, until finally there were just a handful of produce stands holding guard.

Finally, the tide began to turn. One day I showed up and the small spice stand at one end of the piazza had expanded to take over four spaces. Not only was the vendor selling spices, he was now offering olives, dried fruit and nuts, and bags of sun-dried tomatoes and porcini.

Other new arrivals targeted what turned out to be the biggest groups of visitors to the market these days: tourists. Stands selling T-shirts, sun hats, and souvenirs began to fill up other spaces. At the same time, the established fruit and vegetable stands, which offer some of the best (and most expensive) produce in the city, began to get into the game. Not content with merely selling high-end produce to the wealthy residents of Rome's *centro storico*, they also began to turn some of their fruit into fruit salad or fresh juices, which were grabbed up by tourists. Similarly the housewares stand started selling brightly colored ceramics and cute pasta cutters next to the more practical forks and can openers.

The most recent additions to the market are stands that appear to be selling "food" but are really selling "foodlike" souvenirs. Yes, I'm talking about bags of multicolored, anatomically shaped pasta and pink limoncello in violin-shaped bottles. (What is that stuff anyway?)

I admit it would be easy to dismiss the market these days as a purely Disney-like tourist attraction. Yes, there are some stands that are there only to make a profit by selling strange "foodlike" products and souvenirs to tourists. But the seven or eight stands that still sell produce are among the best in Rome. During a recent visit I saw plump strawberries from Terracina; beautiful flower-bedecked *zucchini romanesco*; pencil-thin wild asparagus; and what were probably some of the only wild *ovoli* mushrooms on sale in Rome that day. These were all being sold by the same families who have been standing behind their fruits and vegetables for generations.

No, it's not a farmers' market, and no, it's not necessarily local and almost never organic. But in the age when open markets are a dying breed, I'm just happy to see a market still there. And if some of the icky stuff for sale can help subsidize the truly excellent produce side of things, then I think that is a good thing. Sadly, not all markets can be farmers' markets.

There has been an open-air market in Campo de' Fiori for hundreds of years. And I'm pretty sure that centuries ago, there were stands that were selling schlock stuff, too. Things change, for better and for worse. And, at the end of the day, if the changes that have gone on and continue to go on in Campo de' Fiori mean that the market still exists, then I'm all for change. A changed market is better than no market at all.

shopping lesson

Perhaps my affection for Campo de' Fiori comes from the fact that I truly learned how to shop here. One thing that it took me years to master was market etiquette. I'm not talking about my continued grammatical struggle to learn when to use the formal *Lei* versus the informal *tu*. I'm talking about how to actually get the fruits and vegetables from their place on the stands into my shopping bag. Pick it up and pay for it, you say? Oh, nothing is that easy in Rome

First of all I had to choose which stand to go to. And while you may think that I would just go to one stand that has the ripest tomatoes and then another that has the firmest asparagus, you'd be wrong. Because I learned long ago that once you pick a vendor, you have to stick to her, for better or worse. Yes, kind of like a marriage—or a hairdresser.

If you are only in Rome visiting, and shopping at the market for one day, then this doesn't matter so much. But if you plan on going back, even if it's only for a one-week vacation in Rome, then you'd better pick your vendor and stick to her. Because that is how you are going to end up with the beautifully and perfectly ripe peach that she has hidden away, and not the one with the big bruise.

I learned this the hard way. I'd been doing my shopping at Campo de' Fiori, and had been frequenting mostly one stand, since it seemed to have the best produce and prices. At first the owner was her typically brusque self, not being especially nice, but not being rude either. Just rough. You know, Roman. But I did notice that even if her demeanor didn't much improve, every time I went back I would come away with better and better produce. At first I would inevitably find at least one iffy piece of something at the bottom of my bag: a slightly bruised apple, an overripe pear, or a totally green plum that would never ripen. But slowly, I realized that this wasn't happening anymore. Rather than fill my bags with the produce on display in the front crates, my lady would head to the back, to slip in the premium produce. The stuff she keeps hidden and reserves for her regular customers. While I kind of understood what was happening, and was very glad to be considered a regular, I didn't fully realize that there were certain rules I had to play along with.

One day I made the mistake of coming to the market with an actual shopping list (I was making something slightly complicated for a dinner party). Since my *fruttivendolo* didn't have the asparagus that the soup required, I thought, "no problem," I'll just head two stands down and pick up two beautiful bunches I'd seen earlier.

It wasn't a problem at all until I returned home from a shopping trip to the market two days later and found, once again, a completely bug-ridden tomato at the bottom of my bag. A not so gentle reminder from my *signora* that (a) she saw me cheating on her, and (b) I'd better not do it again if I expected to be treated in the manner to which I had so blissfully accustomed myself.

At this point you may be thinking, Why don't you just choose your own fruit and vegetables? That way you could just get what you'd like. Well, I have one thing to say to you: *non toccare!* That means "don't touch," or rather "DON'T TOUCH," since that phrase is almost always screamed in a way that shames you into never fondling anyone else's peaches in public ever again.

How do you figure out if the fruit is ripe?

The simple answer is you don't. You must put yourself blindly in the hands of the vendor. Show loyalty, and she'll give you the good stuff. Cross her? Well, that bruised banana can always go into a fruit salad.

Another thing I love about the markets in Rome is the convenience. I'm obviously not talking about walking to the market during its limited opening hours and making my way home lugging bags. I'm talking about buying vegetables prepped and ready to cook.

In the States, part of the debate about trying to get people to eat more vegetables has to do with the fact that vegetables are time-consuming to prepare. That when faced with something like an artichoke, asparagus, or even a head of lettuce, many Americans can't be bothered to clean, trim, and cook. The processed alternative is to buy a bag of prewashed lettuce, "mini" carrots, or frozen spinach. But these "vegetables," which have been prepped in huge factories, long after they have been picked, have about as much flavor and nutritional value as a shoe insert. It's no wonder that so many people say they don't like vegetables.

This is why I'm so happy/lucky to live in Italy. Yes, I'm as lazy as the next person. Come mealtime, it's not as if I always have the time/energy/patience to shell 3 kilos of peas, trim a dozen artichokes, or—I admit it—even peel a carrot. The great thing is that I don't have to. Vegetable vendors in Italy are only too happy to do the dirty work for you. Go to any open-air market, or even a local vegetable store, and you'll see baskets of trimmed and washed greens, bags of *cipolline* (onions) or shelled fava beans, all prepared daily by the vendors themselves.

My favorites are the mixes. Each market stand or vegetable store has its own spin on minestrone and salad, which change with the season. Pumpkin is sold in large wedges, so you can buy just what you need. Beans are freshly shelled, green beans trimmed and bagged and ready for steaming. Even wild chicory is neatly trimmed of its dirty roots, so all you have to do is give it a rinse before cooking.

Watching the vendors clean the vegetables is also a nifty and free culinary lesson. Stop by any morning, and you'll see older men and women sitting next to piles of produce, trimming away with plastic-handled, dull-looking knives. Some wear gloves, but most have hands weathered and scarred by decades of nipping and cutting.

Besides teaching you how to clean a vegetable, the vendors are always happy to provide a recipe. In fact, some of my favorite recipes have come from conversations started over piles of beans, cabbage, and squash. Over the years I've learned that if I don't recognize a vegetable, I needn't worry about how to prepare it. A simple *"Come se fa?"* ("How do you do it?") usually results not only in the fruttivendolo giving me her favorite recipe, but, nine times out of ten, the other women waiting patiently for their turn will also chime in. Before I know it, I'm the focus of a lively discussion on the merits of whether to roast or braise, garlic versus onion, or the dilemma of deciding to make a soup or pasta.

Try having that experience in a supermarket.

when in rome . . .

- Don't touch before you buy. Let the fruit and vegetable vendor fill your basket.

- Be true to your vendor. Loyalty to your chosen stand will always get you the best produce.

- If you don't know, ask. Vendors often have the best recipes.

- Watch and learn. Most vendors will let you watch while they prep the vegetables for sale.

- Don't bargain. It's just not done.

favorite markets in rome

Farmers' Market at Circo Massimo
Via di San Teodoro 74
Saturday, 9:00 a.m. to 5:00 p.m. and
Sunday, 9:00 a.m. to 2:00 p.m.
➤ This is a true farmers' market, with only local produce grown in Lazio. Lately, this is where I do most of my weekly shopping.

Campo de' Fiori Market

Piazza Campo de' Fiori
Monday through Saturday,
7:00 a.m. to 2:00 p.m.

➤ This is one of the few remaining outdoor markets in the center of Rome. Yes, it's full of junk, but it also has some of the best produce in the city.

Testaccio

Via Galvani 57
Monday through Saturday,
7:00 a.m. to 2:00 p.m.

➤ One of the best markets in Rome, it has recently moved to a modern building, but is still home to some of the best vendors in town. Everything from meat and fish to fruit, vegetables, and even wine. Located near the old slaughterhouse, Testaccio also sells a wide array of offal and even horse meat, in case you are in the market for this.

Nuovo Mercato Esquilino

Via Principe Amadeo 184
Monday, Wednesday, Thursday,
Saturday, 5:00 a.m. to 3:00 p.m.; Tuesday
and Friday, 5:00 a.m. to 5:00 p.m.

➤ This is Rome's ethnic market, and is lively, colorful, and full of hard-to-find things like mangoes, yams, and lemongrass. It has one of the best fish markets in town.

Trionfale Market

Via la Goletta 1

Monday through Saturday, 7:00 a.m. to 2:00 p.m.; Tuesday and Friday, open until 7:00 p.m.

➤ The Trionfale market is not only Rome's biggest, it's one of the biggest in Italy. With more than 270 vendors, you can find just about everything here. Located in a heavily residential neighborhood near the Vatican, it is one of the most authentic in Rome.

recipes

minestrone

Serves 4 to 6

I can't remember the last time I made minestrone from scratch. And by scratch I mean buy each vegetable separately and chop it up. I do, however, buy bags full of prechopped fresh minestrone mix at the market almost every week. More or less, this is the recipe I follow.

> ¼ cup (60 milliliters) extra-virgin olive oil
> 1 onion, chopped
> 1 teaspoon salt
> 4 garlic cloves, finely chopped
> 2 pounds (1 kilo) mixed fresh vegetables, which should include the following:
> > • carrots
> > • cabbage
> > • zucchini
> > • celery
> > • bell peppers
> > • tomatoes
> > • potatoes
> >
> > (But really, you can add green beans, pumpkin, leeks, cauliflower, broccoli, kale. They are all good.)

Heat the olive oil in a large soup pot over medium heat. Add the onion and salt and cook until softened, about 10 minutes

Add the garlic to the onion and cook for about 8 minutes, or until softened but not browned.

Add the chopped vegetables and stir well. If using bulky greens like Swiss chard, put a lid on the pot and let them wilt for about 5 minutes, then add the remaining vegetables.

Remove the lid, add enough water to cover by one inch, and cook slowly for about 1 hour. When the soup has finished cooking, blend with an immersion blender for a couple of seconds just to thicken up the broth a bit; you still want the soup to be chunky. Taste and correct for salt.

Of course you can play around with the ingredients. And feel free to throw in an old piece of Parmesan rind, which will add extra flavor.

vignarola

Serves 4

Romans still eat very seasonally. They are wary of strawberries except for a few short weeks a year, and gobble up as much *puntarelle* (chicory) as they can during its brief season, only two months in winter.

When it comes to seasonal vegetables, nothing beats the holy trinity of artichokes, fava beans, and peas. They each have their own specific time: First the huge purple romanesco artichokes start showing up. Then the bright green, bursting-at-the-seams fava pods. And finally, just before the favas leave the stage, peas make their entrance. The result is one of Rome's most loved—but maybe least known—dishes: *vignarola*.

I have never seen this dish on a menu outside of Rome, much less outside of Italy. Maybe that is because its success has as much to do with the freshest ingredients as with any culinary skill. The artichokes that grow in Lazio are unique. And the dish is made with very fresh, very young fava beans that require no double shelling. Hard to find in most places.

But I also think that one of the reasons that vignarola is not on any menus is due to the fact that it is so damn labor-intensive. While easy to cook, the vegetables themselves take forever to prep. Shelling enough favas and peas for a meal for four can take you a half hour. Then there are the artichokes, which must be shorn of their tough outer leaves, trimmed around the root, dechoked, and sliced, all the while keeping them (and your hands) in an

acidulated bath so that they don't turn brown. But, if you are lucky enough to live in Rome, then you can pick up tidy little packages of fresh shelled peas and fava beans and trimmed artichokes in the markets around town.

¼ cup (60 milliliters) extra-virgin olive oil

3 scallions (white parts only)

6 artichokes, tough outer leaves and choke removed, cleaned and sliced

2 cups shelled fava beans

Salt

Freshly ground black pepper

3 cups (¾ liter) water, or more as needed

1½ cups shelled peas

2 cups finely chopped romaine lettuce

Heat the oil in a large pot, add the scallions, and gently soften without browning. Add the artichokes and stir a bit, then stir in the fava beans. Season with salt and pepper, and add about 3 cups of water. Cover and simmer for about 40 minutes, adding more water if necessary; you want it to be somewhere between a soup and a stew. Add the peas and lettuce and cook for another 8 to 10 minutes. Taste and correct for salt.

Depending on how I'm feeling, I sometimes add chopped guanciale or pancetta at the beginning with the scallions. Another option is to add fresh mint or parsley at the very end. If I'm feeling particularly daring, I add some grated lemon zest, which is completely untraditional.

please do not eat within ten feet of any monument

oday's Roman food lesson involves eating in the street. Don't do it. Actually, it's pretty much a lesson you can take with you all over Italy. If you are American then this may come as a bit of a shock. People do not buy sandwiches, bags of chips, cans of soda, and cups of coffee and eat or drink them in public. In fact, eating in public is as sure a way to shout, "Hey, I'm American" as wearing flip-flops and shorts to visit the Vatican.

In fact, there was a recent law passed in Rome aimed specifically at tourists. No eating anything within ten feet of any historic monument. Since Rome is basically one big historic monument, that pretty much meant no eating anything, anywhere, anytime outdoors. While the law was a bit draconian (and almost impossible to enforce), the general understanding was that it was aimed at uncouth foreigners who would (at least in theory) be eating whole chickens on the Spanish Steps and leaving greasy bones behind.

Of course, nothing of the sort ever happened, and if the city of Rome was leery of garbage piling up it could of course have resolved the situation with, say, a few garbage cans and/or street cleaners rather than bringing in the armed guard. But anyway, the fact that the city thought that eating in the street was actually a criminal act gives you some sort of idea just how seriously Italians take this eating-in-the-street thing.

Basically, it's just considered bad form. And think about it. Do you actually like to see (and smell) someone chowing down on a Greek salad or a pastrami sandwich on the seat across from you on the subway? No, you don't. It's just not *bella figura,* as the Romans say. Especially in public, you must put your most elegantly shod foot forward.

But as with everything Italian, every rule has its huge gaping exceptions (which is why you need this book to help navigate the sometimes treacherous food landscape). So, to repeat, never ever eat in the street.

Unless, of course, it is either gelato or pizza bianca.

Gelato is, of course, the understandable exception. A cone, or small paper cup, is made for walking around with. In fact, head out into Rome for a late-afternoon stroll on a Sunday, around 5:00 p.m., and you'd swear there was actually a fine for not having an ice cream cone in your hand.

Pizza bianca is a bit more difficult to understand. Pizza bianca is just what it sounds like: "white pizza." In other words, this is pizza dough, baked, with nothing more than olive oil on it. It is not the pizza you order in a restaurant. Nor is it *pizza al taglio,* or "pizza by the slice." (See chapter 23.)

The recipe for pizza bianca is one of those simple ones that depend completely on the quality of the ingredients: flour, water, and yeast. And the best pizza bianca is made with a yeast starter that has been going for decades and gives each one its unique flavor. Then there is the olive oil, which has to be good, too, and the rising time.

The best pizza bianca in Rome is left to rise overnight. The *fornaio,* "baker," comes in about 7:00 in the morning and begins his daylong job of stretching the 30-inch ball of dough over the length of a 5-foot board. Using delicate hands, he (yes, the bakers are always male) tries to retain most of the original air bubbles that have formed overnight. He then gently brushes on a coating of olive oil, and slips the dough in the oven. He then repeats this process every 10 to 20 minutes all day long.

Why? Because pizza bianca has a shelf life of about 45 minutes. You want it so hot you can barely hold it when you buy it, because in about an hour it will lose its soft, chewy yet crunchy, oily, salty texture and become something cold, hard, and tough.

Which explains why, if you stand outside of a bakery in Rome—like Il Forno Campo de' Fiori or Roscioli—you will see all manner of people coming out of the shop with a square of pizza bianca, wrapped with a piece of paper to protect their hands, as they—yes—eat it in the street while walking away. Women in chic dresses and high heels, men in three-piece suits, garbage collectors on their break, mothers pushing prams. While any and all of them would look with disdain at a foreigner doing the same thing with a sandwich or bottle of Coke, pizza bianca is a completely different story.

Why? Because you have to eat it when it is hot. That is when it is best, and if you wait until you take it home, it will completely lose any of its appeal.

Like any good Roman mother, I handed pizza bianca to Emma and Sophie in their strollers as one of their first snacks. Or, should I say, it was one of the first snacks other people gave to my children. Walk into almost any bakery with a child in a stroller and before anyone else is waited on, the person behind the counter will come around and hand over a strip of pizza just big enough to be held in a chubby fist.

The first time this happened I was a bit worried. Was one-year-old Sophie ready for pizza? Was it too salty? Too greasy? Were her little teeth poorly equipped to handle the chewy treat? I should have known better. Sophie, like all good little Roman children, chomped down on her prize and hasn't let go since.

There is, of course, one other major way that Romans eat in the streets: seated at restaurants. And in fact, there are few things more magical than sitting in the shade on a warm spring day, or enjoying the cooling breezes on a hot summer night, while enjoying a plate of pasta and a bottle of wine. Yet once again, arcane Italian laws paired with rising real estate prices and the increasing tide of tourists mean that outdoor tables and good food is a combination that is oddly hard to find these days in Rome.

When I first lived in Rome in the 1970s, I remember two types of outdoor-dining experiences. While there were fancy restaurants, like Piperno and Pierluigi, that had very formal setups outside their restaurants, complete with starched white tablecloths and crisply dressed waiters, there were also plenty of more casual options.

I distinctly remember rickety wooden tables being crammed onto narrow sidewalks, to allow trattoria diners to take advantage of eating *al fresco* whenever weather permitted. These impromptu setups felt a bit like a cross between a picnic and a restaurant, and the precariousness, combined with just being outside, always made the food taste better.

These days the "occupation of public space" is a tightly controlled commodity. A combination of increased taxes and trying to cut down on the encroachment of pubs and bars onto every square inch of every piazza means that some of the best—and simplest—places can't afford to have tables outside anymore.

One of the things I wish Rome would take more advantage of is the enormous amount of gorgeous open and green space. Rome has got to be one of the greenest cities I know, with countless beautiful parks and the Tiber running right through its heart. But unlike Paris, which sets up great ways to enjoy the riverside and the *jardins* with bars and restaurants, Rome's amenities usually leave a bit to be desired. While there could—and should—be outdoor eateries in the parks yearlong, at least in the summer things change for the better.

One of my favorite places to go for dinner in the summer is the Festa dell'Unita. It used to be the annual Communist festival, but is today run by the Left-leaning party *du jour*. It's hard to keep up with yearly political changes, but we ignore all that and just go for the food. There are usually about fifteen restaurants set up, some big, some small. Prices are low, and the variety huge: Middle Eastern, paella, Calabrian, fish, grilled meats, Roman Jewish plus a handful of pastry and ice cream places. We usually stop by the Cuban (Communist!) booth for a surprisingly good piña colada. My favorite is always the stand run by the organic cooperative that delivers my CSA produce, Agricultura Nuova. It always has a huge and very elaborate grill going, so sausages feature prominently. Until recently the fair was held not too far from the Colosseum. Lately it's been located a bit farther afield, near San Paolo Fuori le Mure.

Another summer event takes place near the river and takes over the banks of Tiber Island. Although the event's main attraction is an outdoor cinema festival, the restaurants and bars that spread out along the river offer some of the most dramatic and breeze-filled settings in which to dine and drink in Rome. The concessions change each year, but the dreamy location—along the banks of the roaring Tiber—remains romantically unchanged.

My favorite Roman outdoor eating experiences though are the small neighborhood festivals that used to be common and are now, unfortunately, a dying breed. Rome is divided into neighborhoods, or rioni, and each one typically had its own festival. Historically, the one in Testaccio had the reputation of being particularly raucous. Evidently part of celebrations in the eighteenth century included launching a cart full of pigs down the steep incline of the Testaccio hill. As the cart picked up speed, drunken (and evidently hungry) revelers would trail after it, until it—and they—finally crashed at the bottom. The winners came out of the Bacchanalian melee with a pig as their prize. Don't worry, things have toned down a bit.

The festivals are much like the *sagre* that take place in small villages all over Italy. The starting point is a saint's name day and, after a brief Mass and the walking of a statue of a patron saint through the streets, the festival begins. The most famous of the festivals in recent years is the Festa de' Noantri in Trastevere. The name of the festival, *noantri*, is Roman slang and translates roughly as "us others," referring to the people living on the other side of the river (*Trastevere* means "other side of the

Tiber") as somehow a breed apart from Romans. The *festa* begins with the parade of the Beatra Vergine del Carmelo through the streets on July 15. The weeklong festival used to be a Roman party involving the entire neighborhood, but seems to have quieted down with the lack of interest from local shopkeepers.

Instead, the Ottobrata Monticiana, which takes place in the neighborhood of Monti, is a newer festival. Founded about twenty-five years ago to instill a sense of neighborhood pride in Rome's oldest rione, the Ottobrata is currently enjoying a tremendous popularity. Twenty-five years ago it was founded and supported purely by local families who had grown up and lived here all their lives. Today, with the gentrification of the neighborhood, business owners are joining in the fun, and have turned it into a three-night-long block party. Local families set up in the parish kitchen where they turn out such Roman specialties as tripe, amatriciana, and grilled sausages. You can take your plates full of steaming goodness and try to nab one of the few rickety picnic tables set up along Via Baccina. Or else play fast and loose with the laws and sit yourself down on the steps of the sixteenth-century fountain in the square. It's OK. You'll probably be sitting next to the local police, who have long since stopped enforcing the "don't eat in the street" law. I mean, really!

eating pizza bianca in rome

It's a toss-up who has the best pizza bianca in Rome. Certainly there are local bakeries that are making excellent examples, but these two centrally located bakeries get a lot of attention. This is partly due to their excellent pizza, and partly due to their location. I would advise you to make your own informed decision, by visiting each one at least five times.

Roscioli
Via dei Chiavari 34
➤ Considered one of the best bakeries in town, they are known as much for their crusty loaves as for their excellent pizza bianca.

Il Forno Campo de' Fiori
Campo de' Fiori 22
➤ At this bakery, famous for pizza bianca, you can watch it being made at their store-front window all day long.

Panificio Bonci
Via Trionfale 34
and Pizzarium
Via della Meloria 43
➤ Perhaps the best pizza bianca in town, it is made by Gabriele Bonci, who has been referred to as the Michelangelo of pizza. His technique has transformed the way people think about this humble street food. (See page 213.)

my favorite outdoor restaurants

Sometimes food just tastes better when you're sitting outside. There are certain times of the year when I'll head to a restaurant as much for the chance to enjoy my meal al fresco as for the food. The following places are some of my favorites:

Pierluigi
Piazza Ricci, 39-06-6861-302

➤ I admit that I love this place as much for the setting as for the food. The tranquil sixteenth-century piazza is almost like a movie set it's so perfect. The food, which is mostly fish, is also pretty great. While the restaurant used to be formal, but simple, it's recently gone more upscale. The food is still excellent (even better), but you definitely pay the price. An added bonus is the excellent cocktail service.

Giggetto
Via Portico d'Ottavia 21a, 39-06-686-1105

➤ Don't look to Giggetto for fancy or creative. Do run here for all the Roman classics—amatriciana, carbonara, and gricia are all excellent. I've been going here since I was twelve, and it's still one of my favorites. And the outdoor setting, beneath the Roman Portico d'Ottavia, is dreamy.

Flavio Velavevodetto
Via di Monte Testaccio 97, 39-06-574-4194

➤ In the winter months I usually head to Perilli for my classic Roman Testaccio fix of amatriciana and carbonara. But once the weather turns warm enough, I love Flavio's

rooftop terrace. Make sure you ask for the upper terrace, which looks over mostly green fields across the street.

outdoor festivals in rome

Festa del Cinema Isola Tiberina

➢ This outdoor festival is set up on the banks of the Tiber Island and usually runs from June 1 to August 31. The restaurants change yearly. I'd recommend getting there early enough to stop by one of the bars for an *aperitivo,* then dinner at one of the half dozen restaurants.

Festa dell'Unita

➢ Just Google the name of this political festival, Festa dell'Unita, to find out the current location. Most recently it was in Parco Shuster in front of the Basilica di San Paolo. The yearly festival takes place over the entire month of July and offers a big selection of fun outdoor places to eat dinner. It's a bit chaotic, so arrive on the early side.

Ottobrata Monticiana, Rione Monti

➢ This neighborhood festival usually takes place the second or third weekend of October. Each year is different, but there is usually a rustic restaurant set up on Via Baccina, where you can enjoy plastic plates full of amatriciana, tripe, and stewed beans. Last year's festival also included events on Via Urbana.

when in rome . . . rules for eating outside

- There are only two socially accepted things to eat while walking: gelato and pizza bianca.

- Don't have a picnic on the steps of a church or fountain, or you may get arrested.

- If you feel like having a picnic, stock up and head for one of Rome's many public parks.

- If you're seated at a restaurant outside make sure you keep an eye on your handbag. Just saying.

recipes

fagioli con le cotiche
{ beans with pork rind }

Serves 6

If you've ever been to a street festival in Rome, there are two items that are sure to be on the menu: sausages and beans. The sausages will usually be grilled, while the beans are cooked long and slow with the addition of big pieces of *cotiche*, or "pig skin." At the Ottobrata Monticiana they serve both of these. All of the dishes are cooked by women who

(continued)

live in the neighborhood, and who spend days preparing the food. I'm pretty sure that one of the reasons the beans tasted so good was that these kinds of dishes always improve in flavor if they are made the day before.

> 1 pound (500 grams) dried cannellini beans
>
> Salt
>
> ¼ pound (250 grams) pork rind
>
> 2 celery stalks
>
> 1 whole peeled onion
>
> 1 garlic clove
>
> ¼ cup extra-virgin olive oil
>
> 1 small onion, chopped
>
> 3 stalks celery, chopped
>
> 2 garlic cloves, chopped
>
> 4 cups (500 grams) canned tomato puree

Soak the beans overnight. On the following day, cook them in abundant salted water until tender and cooked through.

Prepare the pork rind: Parboil the rind for about 8 minutes in boiling water. Drain and cut it into thin strips. If you don't want it too fatty, you can trim off some of the fat. Place the strips into a pot and cover with cold water. Add the celery stalks, whole onion, and garlic clove and bring to a simmer. Let cook for 1 to 1½ hours until the pork is very tender. Drain the pork rind, reserving some of the cooking liquid.

Heat the olive oil in a large pot, add the chopped onion, celery, and garlic, and cook until softened, about 10 minutes. Add the tomato puree and cook briskly until the sauce thickens.

Add the drained pork rind and let it cook for another 10 minutes or so. Add the cooked beans and a bit of the bean or pork rind cooking liquid if it seems too dry. Cook for another 20 to 30 minutes.

This dish is even better if you serve it on the following day.

umberto's funghi porcini

Serves 6

Umberto lives just down the street from me. He is an ex-professional boxer and now has a small secondhand junk store. I know he must be doing something else in there, but the front has more tchotchkes than you've ever seen in your life. One day he knocked on my door and wanted to know if I'd be moving my car anytime soon, since he was having a dinner party that night.

Yup, he sets up a table right in the street. Our neighborhood, Monti, is really like a small village and life goes on as much in the street as behind closed doors. A life that includes eating, despite the recent law passed by the intensely moronic current government that bans eating outside on or near anything historic. Evidently Umberto didn't get that memo.

So after I moved my car, I decided to visit Umberto and see what he was cooking for his dinner/act of insubordination in progress. Umberto had been to the market that morning, and picked up a kilo of *funghi porcini* and some sausages, which he was cooking in his makeshift kitchen. His other guests were bringing fruit, side dishes, and even an Indonesian stir-fry.

Later that night as I headed home from a dinner party at my neighbor's, I stopped by to say hello. The sausages and mushrooms were long gone, but the wine was still flowing, and would be for a few more hours yet. Umberto and his guests were happily parked for the rest of the evening. When I asked them if they were worried about the new law and getting a fine, they all just laughed. I told you they'd all lived here a long time. They knew. Laws come and go, and life pretty much just goes on as it always has.

2 pounds (1 kilo) fresh porcini mushrooms

4 tablespoons extra-virgin olive oil

Salt

Freshly ground black pepper

3 garlic cloves, chopped

1 cup chopped fresh flat-leaf parsley

Trim and clean the mushrooms, using a small brush to wipe away the grit. (You should never use water to clean mushrooms, since this will result in mushy mushrooms when cooked.) Cut the mushrooms into large chunks.

Heat the olive oil in a pan large enough to hold all the mushrooms in one layer. Add the mushrooms and cook on medium-high heat, trying not to stir, for at least the first 7 minutes or so. Then, using the handle of the pan, just jiggle them around a bit, seasoning them with the salt and pepper. When they are well browned, after about 12 minutes or so, add the chopped garlic and stir to combine. Cook for 2 minutes more, then sprinkle with the parsley and serve.

not one-stop shopping

still remember clearly the first time I came down to Rome, from Florence, to stay with Domenico. His apartment, where we still live, was in the Monti neighborhood. Although I had been there in the past to visit Michelangelo's *Moses* and a sixteenth-century church designed by Giacomo della Porta, I didn't really know the area like I did other parts of Rome around Campo de' Fiori and the Jewish Ghetto.

That first day, when Domenico went off to work, I told him I'd do the shopping for dinner. Not really knowing where any shops were, I figured I'd start where it made most sense: in the main Piazza della Madonna dei Monti. And, in fact, not only were there two vegetable stores to choose from, there was also a flower stand, a newspaper stand, and a dusty but delicious-looking pastry shop. Just up the main street of Via dei Serpenti, I discovered two different *alimentari*, two bread bakeries, and a fish store. Off of nearby alleys I had three butcher shops to choose from.

That day I came home with two pork chops cut to order, some *broccolo romano*, and potatoes, and as a special treat two sour cherry turnovers that were still warm from the oven. Over the next few months, as my trips down to Rome from Florence became more and more frequent, I not only fell in love with Domenico, whom I would soon marry, but also began a relationship with the owners of the neighborhood shops.

While my marriage with Domenico is still going strong, little did I know that in terms of my daily shopping routine I was falling in love with a way of life that was sadly on its last legs. The prevalence of small family-owned specialty shops all over Rome—and Italy, for that matter—used to be the norm. Each neighborhood had its share of butchers and bakers and—at least when I first moved here—there were still several candlestick makers.

Although I didn't realize it at the time, I had moved into an area of Rome that was still inhabited by the same people who had grown up here. The gentrification and increasing levels of tourism, which led to astronomical increases in real estate prices, hadn't quite hit Monti yet. Obviously, since we were living there, we ourselves represented change. But when Sophie and Emma first started kindergarten at the local school, we, as "outsiders," were still very much in the minority. The parents of Sophie's classmates were the same people I had been seeing every day. They owned the bakery and the bar, the shoe store and the pastry shop. Their parents had owned these places before them and, for the most part, at least in the beginning, they weren't complaining.

But slowly things began to change. One of the first casualties was the corner pastry shop. Once the mother who had run it died, the son decided to move to an area of Rome where the rents were less expensive. Similar fates befell the bakery, two of the butchers, and one of the alimentari.

One of the few survivors of the old guard is the butcher located at the corner of Via Panisperna and Via del Boschetto. It is barely big enough for one meat-packed counter, and there is no real sign outside, just red tape used to spell out the word *macelleria*. In fact, a lot of people who go there don't even know that the name of the owner is Piero Stecchiotti. Why he has persevered where others have failed has a bit to do with survival of the fittest—or the highest quality. Because rather than try to compete with cheaper and more convenient supermarkets, Stecchiotti has steadfastly stuck to his original principles of quality. With no compromises, his meat is among the best in Rome. It is also the most expensive.

And today, that is how small stores in Rome still manage to get by. Yes, there are a lot fewer of them, but the ones that do survive often do so by offering something unique and of extraordinary quality. At the same time a younger generation is beginning to open new specialty shops that focus on those same qualities.

new speciality stores

Aromaticus
Via Urbana 134, 39-06-488-1355
➤ If I could dream up the kind of shop I would want someone to open in Monti, I'd imagine a place where I could buy fresh herb plants—from wild cress and mint to

Sicilian oregano and French tarragon, and peppers from all over the world, lemongrass, and little pots of mustard sprouts. I'd also like to be able to sit down to eat: nothing heavy, just enough for a lunch or teatime. And if there could be a section devoted to spices and garden supplies that would be nice, too. That about sums up Aromaticus, the newest arrival on Via Urbana.

Emporio delle Spezie

Via Luca della Robbia 20, 39-327-861-2655
➤ This pocket-sized store is tucked into a side street in Testaccio. Crystal-clear jars line the shelves, filled with more than 150

spices from all over the world. While the owner certainly has Italian things like hot peppers and saffron, she's also up on peppers from Sarawak, salts from Hawaii, and any other Indian spice I could ever dream of needing.

D.O.L.

Via Panaroli 35, 39-06-243-00765
➤ This shop specializes in hard-to-find, traditionally made cheeses, cured meats, olives, and other regional specialties. Acting almost as an outlet for these food artisans, cutting out any middleman and markup, the shop features the kinds of

foods that usually don't make it much beyond their villages, much less into Rome. The result of this exhaustive sourcing and minimal markup is, I can safely say, some of the most absurdly delicious food in Rome at almost ridiculously low prices. Located in a neighborhood far from the center of Rome, it is well worth the trip.

Beppe e i suoi Formaggi

Via Santa Maria del Pianto 9A/11, 39-06-6819-2210

➤ Beppe e i suoi Formaggi ("Beppe and His Cheeses") is the newest arrival on the cheese scene in Rome, and a welcome addition, since great cheeses are oddly difficult to find in this city. Cheeses are very regional in Italy, and some of the very best come from Piedmonte. As does Beppe himself. Beppe (Giuseppe) Giovale is a cheese producer, whose shop features what may be the most delicious selection of cheeses from Piedmonte in Rome. The large counter runs the length of the store and is filled with goat, sheep, and cow's milk cheeses. The back wall is a beautiful "cave" piled high with entire wheels.

traditional speciality shops

Moriondo e Gariglio

Via Piè di Marmo 21–22, 39-06-699-0856

➤ Rome's most famous chocolate shop, it is also its most beautiful. Walls covered in red satin and foil-covered bonbons glittering on the shelves make the place feel like a jewel box. Moriondo e Gariglio has been hand-crafting chocolates since 1870 and continues to do so with passion. Their filled chocolates are what most people come for— small confections filled with only the freshest ingredients; they have a shelf life of only a few days, so it is best to eat them yourself, rather than bring them back as gifts! My favorites include caffè, hazelnut, and pistachio, but what brings me back every fall are the magnificent candied chestnuts— huge and glistening with sugary sweetness. If you happen by before Easter, you will see the elaborately decorated Easter eggs. These are made to order, and they are happy to include a surprise of your choosing on the inside. And in winter, have a seat at one of two tables and settle in for a cup of hot chocolate—pure molten heaven.

Norcineria Viola

Piazza Campo de' Fiori 43, 39-06-688-06114

➤ Even if the market at Campo de' Fiori has grown smaller and a bit more touristy over the last decade, Norcineria Viola is one of the serious food vendors that still holds its place in one of the buildings that line the square. Norcineria Viola has been going at it for more than a century. They sell one thing, and one thing only: cured pork. But if you think that narrows the range of what's on offer, think again. Any size, shape, or variety of cured pork they've got: *prosciutti,* salami, guanciale, and pancetta for sure. And also about twenty kinds of salame from all over Italy: dozens of types of prosciutti; big fat slabs of glistening lard; jelly-laden pigs' feet. They even have pastrami from up north. OK, that's beef masquerading as cured pork, but the rest of the shop is pork and pork only—a veritable shrine to pork.

Volpetti

Via Marmorata 47, 39-06-574-2352

➤ If you care about food and are in Rome (and if you're reading this, that's a given), then making a pilgrimage to Volpetti, the temple of *gastronomia* in Rome, is a must. The Volpetti brothers, Emilio and Claudio, have made an art out of sourcing the best cheeses, cured meats, and other delicacies throughout Italy and bringing them to their shop, where they not only sell them, but educate their clients with joy and enthusiasm.

It's difficult to enter into the shop without having someone immediately offer you a taste of whatever has just arrived. It may be an aged ham from Trentino or a goat's milk *caprino* from Piedmonte. Whatever it is, chances are you'll end up buying some

and taking home not only something good to eat, but also a new taste experience.

Nowadays Volpetti works directly with certain producers, procuring hard-to-find cheeses, made to order and aged in their own cheese cellar. The mozzarella, which is delivered straight from Campania, is possibly the best in Rome. Be forewarned: Before you get caught up in a buying frenzy, remember quality doesn't come cheaply, or you'll have sticker shock when you check out.

La Tradizione

Via Cipro 8, 39-06-397-20349

➤ Some people call La Tradizione the "Temple of Cheese." I'm not going to argue with them. I've tried to count the number of cheeses they carry, but always give up after about fifty. And it's not the numbers that count anyway, it's the quality. There is, bar none, no better cheese store in Rome. Misters Fantucci and Belli have been running things here for about thirty years, and the selection and quality only grow. They not only carry the biggest selection of Italian cheeses, but include a hefty number of foreign cheeses, too.

how to order coffee like a roman

One of the most difficult things I had to get used to when I moved full time to Italy as a graduate student was the whole coffee thing. I moved to Florence to work on my dissertation on sixteenth-century Italian gardens. This meant that, between undergraduate and graduate work, I had been studying for about eight years, and much of those eight years had been spent drinking coffee.

Whether I was in a lecture hall, in a library, or just studying at home there was almost always a large cup of caffeine near at hand. Part of this was all about the stimulant, of course. Another lecture about seventeenth-century Dutch triptychs? Fill 'er up.

But once I got to Italy, I realized that the hot cup of coffee almost constantly within reach was only marginally about helping me stay awake. The differences in coffee culture between Italy and the States were my wake-up call (sorry, pun sort of intended) for deep-seated cultural differences when it came to food.

The thing is, I knew Italy. I was no novice getting a new passport for her first trip abroad. I'd been coming here for about twenty years, for god's sake. But when I realized that I couldn't stop by a coffee shop on my way to the library and get a large coffee to go to see me through the morning, I felt as if someone had taken away something essential to my soul.

I would find myself sitting in the library, working my way through a report on a sixteenth-century Medici shopping list, and my hand would reach out, blindly searching for the coffee that wasn't there. It was like feeling a missing limb. It was painful.

That's when I realized that when it came to eating and drinking, I was still pretty much American in my lack of discipline. What I soon learned was that when it came to food in Italy, there were a lot of rules regarding what you consumed, and where and when.

Getting back to coffee. In America coffee is pretty much an all-day affair. Yes, it's something to start your day with. But after that? All rules fly out the window. Even before Starbucks came along, you could always get a cup of coffee at the local diner, deli, or Dunkin' Donuts.

To go.

In Italy I learned the words "coffee" and "to go" don't even exist on a conceptual level.

Like much else about eating and drinking in Italy, coffee has a lot of "rules." And those coffee rules? Well, they change from town to town, region to region—even family to family. So don't think you are ever going to master all of them. You are bound to fail, just don't take it personally.

For instance, in my mother-in-law's eyes, I've been breaking the number one rule of coffee consumption for the last twenty-two years. Domenico's family is from Bari, in the south of Italy. We usually visit at least five or six times a year, and stay in the house where my husband grew up. If you do the math, that means I've woken up and had breakfast with my mother-in-law at least five hundred times, plus another few hundred when she's visited us.

Seven hundred breakfasts? As I pour milk into my coffee to take my first sip of the morning, just as the rim of the coffee cup touches my lip, she says, "What?! You're not having a black espresso first?" Because in her world, in her family, that was the way you started your day. One small, strong, boiling hot cup of coffee—black, with no sugar. Any other way? Well, it's just not done. (Unless you are the American daughter-in-law, I guess.)

Other coffee rules are purely regional. In Sicily it's not only common, but also totally normal to have a fluffy brioche stuffed with *granita di caffè* for breakfast. Yup. A sweet roll filled with frozen coffee and whipped cream. In Rome, true Romans drink their coffee out of a small glass, not a ceramic cup. Why? Something about the temperature (it either cools off faster or slower; not sure which). But my husband, who is not from Rome, wouldn't be caught dead drinking his coffee out of a glass. Why? It's too Roman. Go figure.

coffee rules

While some coffee-drinking rules seem to be purely personal, like my mother-in-law's, others fall along broader guidelines. Here are a few to help you not appear like a total fool should you want to order coffee in Italy:

1. *Never drink coffee with milk after noon:* I'm pretty sure this one might even be law. Never, ever order a cappuccino after any meal, lunch or dinner. And it does sort of make sense, up to a certain point. I mean, why would anyone want a glass of milk after a big meal? You're already full (in theory) and milk would just make things harder to digest. Also, if the coffee is supposed to wake you up, then the copious amounts of hot dairy would just have the opposite effect. But then I think, hey, what about that huge cannoli you just ordered? A cup and a half of ricotta cheese? Tell me how that's not interfering with your digestion?

2. *Never order your coffee at the counter and then carry it on your own to a table:* Italian coffee bars have a very strict protocol when serving coffee. Once you walk in, you first go to the person behind the cash register. This person will probably be either on the phone or talking to someone else. The last thing they seem interested in is taking your money. If you do convince them to let you order, they should give you a small receipt, a *scontrino,* for your efforts. Hold on tight to this tiny scrap of paper. It's the only proof you have that you've paid for the coffee you have yet to even order. Make your way over to the bar, and then try to get the *barista's* attention. If you are not a regular (and if you are reading this, you are obviously far from being a regular) this might prove hard to do. The barista is probably having a conversation with the lady at the cash register. Once you've ordered, your coffee should come pretty quickly (these guys are fast). Now, whatever you do, don't pick up your cup and saucer and head to a table to sit down! This time, there is actually a law against this. The price you paid at the cash register was for a coffee meant to be consumed while standing up, at the counter. Why didn't the cashier ask you if you wanted to sit at a table? Because if you had wanted to sit at a table, you would have just gone and sat at a table. And then the waiter would have taken your order there. And you would have paid extra for the service.

    Sound confusing? Don't worry, you're not the only one to make this mistake. In fact, if you're bored, and want to amuse yourself at the expense of others, walk into any coffee bar in central Rome and see this scene played out about once every five minutes.

3. *Don't drink too much coffee:* Most Italians do most things in moderation,

including drinking coffee. *Quanti caffè hai bevuto?* ("How many coffees have you had?") This is a common question to be asked. My husband asks me this all the time. And I swear, when I'm at a bar, getting coffee, I hear this conversation over and over. As far as I can tell, anything beyond the response *solo uno* ("only one") is cause for true alarm. *"Stai attento"* ("be careful") they say. Of what, I'm not quite sure. Having this conversation over and over again? Every day?

4. *There is no takeout:* You may be thinking you can avoid the whole table versus bar thing by asking for a coffee to go, right? Wrong. First of all, bars are not set up for takeout coffee. Every so often you'll see a shopkeeper stopping by to pick up an order for her colleagues back in the store. The barista will carefully fill up several tiny, flimsy plastic cups with about a half inch of coffee. He'll then take about five minutes to carefully cut some little squares of aluminum foil to top each cup. Then another five minutes to twist the foil around the edges, by which time the coffee is good and cold, and, well, each of the shopkeepers could have easily run back and forth to the bar in the time it took him to prepare the cups.

    And that large latte you were thinking you could take out and enjoy on the steps of the Pantheon? Forget about it. Rome recently passed a law that says no eating or drinking on or near public monuments, which pretty much includes every square inch of the city.

ordering coffee

If these rules seem draconian and random, they are. But they shouldn't get in the way of you enjoying some of the best coffee in the world. Once you've decided if you'd like to stand at the counter or sit down at a table, here are some of the ways you can order coffee in Rome:

Caffè. This is what most people order, and is otherwise known as an espresso. This is what most Romans head to their favorite bar to drink. Usually served in a heated ceramic cup, the coffee is usually drunk standing up at the bar. To appear very Roman, order yours *in vetro,* "in a glass."

Caffè Macchiato. Stained coffee. Stained with milk, that is. A short shot of espresso with just a tiny drop of milk. If you want to get particular (and Romans are always so about their coffee), then specify if you'd like it *macchiato caldo* (hot) or *macchiato freddo* (cold). Or, you can be like my husband's partner Corrado. He orders his *tiepido.* Yes. Tepid. Yuck.

Caffè Doppio. I'm pretty sure this double shot of espresso was invented for crazy

Americans, who have no regard for being careful of how much coffee they drink. I order this all the time. I especially like to order it in front of my husband, who is sure I will keel over and die from too much coffee.

Cappuccino. A shot of espresso topped with foamed, hot milk. Again, there are endless variations. For instance, a *cappuccino senza schiuma* is a cappuccino without foam. Not so sure what the point of that is, but it's very popular.

Latte Macchiato. A big glass of warm milk, with just a dash of coffee to stain it, and to take the warm milk taste away. I love *latte macchiato,* since it really is pure comfort food disguised as a coffee drink. In Rome most people consider this a drink for children, or for someone who's not feeling well. Or, in most cases, for Americans who prefer their coffee drinks more milky no matter what time of day it is.

Marocchino. This politically incorrectly named drink is light brown. Just like a Moroccan! It's a shot of espresso, a topping of hot, foamed milk, and a generous sprinkling of cocoa. Since this is always served in a small glass, the milk-lightened coffee is on show, hence the name. Although, I've also seen it called *Moretto,* which means "little black man."

Monachella. This one is called "little nun," which is kind of cute. In this case it's just like a marocchino, but the black man is wearing a wimple in the form of a dollop of whipped cream.

Caffè Shakerato. This is one of my favorite summertime coffee drinks. First of all, I love the name. *Shakerato* is just the Italianized version of "shaken." In this drink a room-temperature shot of espresso is poured into a cocktail shaker with ice and a bit of sugar. After about a minute of vigorous shaking, the creamy, foamy, cold coffee is poured into a stemmed glass.

Granita di caffè. It's difficult to include this treat in a discussion of coffee, since it's more like having an ice cream. The amount of caffeine and sugar in this one packs such a wallop that it will keep you going much longer than any straightforward coffee drink. *Granita di caffè* is black sweetened coffee that has been slowly frozen and broken up so that large frozen coffee crystals form. You order it at a bar and the barista will dig deep into a frozen container sunken into the counter to scoop up the icy treat. Your only decision will be whether to have whipped cream on top and bottom or only on top.

Affogato. Just in case you happen to be in a gelateria that is also a coffee bar, or a coffee bar that is also a gelateria, get one of these. This is a shot of espresso into which a spoonful of gelato has been added. My favorite combo is with *zabaione,* and there is a bar near the Pantheon, Fiocco di Neve, that specializes in this. But really? Feel free to make your own whenever you manage to get coffee and gelato on the table at the same time. Play with your food.

Caffè Corretto. "Corrected" coffee. Corrected with the addition of grappa, that is, or any other alcoholic beverage of your choice. In theory this is a morning pick-me-up, usually drunk by farmers or people working in the market who need something just a bit more than coffee to kick-start their mornings. Why not?

Caffè Americano. This is the coffee that was invented to appease the tourists who come to Rome and can't handle the intense little cups of espresso. It's a shot of espresso that is drawn out with extra water. So in the end, it's kind of like drip coffee, and actually not that bad. And if you really want to drive your Italian friends crazy, order a *caffè americano doppio.* They may even call an ambulance just in case.

five places to drink coffee in rome

Best Granita di Caffè

Tazza d'Oro Via degli Orfani 84,
39-06-678-9792

➤ Tazza d'Oro still roasts their own beans, and their house blend is considered by many to be the best in Rome. When the weather turns hot, Romans line up for a cup full of slushy, icy granita di caffè.

Best Espresso

Sant'Eustachio, Piazza di Sant'Eustachio,
39-06-688-02048

➤ Sant'Eustachio, which also roasts its own beans, has something of a cult following. How do they make their espresso taste so good? It's a mystery, since each shot is pulled behind the privacy of a metal partition. My favorite: *caffè doppio con panna,* a double dose of espresso topped with whipped cream.

Best Caffè Affogato

Fiocco di Neve, Via del Pantheon 51,
39-06-678-6025

➤ Head to the back counter of this anonymous-looking gelateria to enjoy the house specialty: *caffè affogato con zabaione,* a piping hot, intense shot of espresso topped by a small scoop of zabaione gelato.

Oldest Caffè in Town

Caffè Greco, Via Condotti 86, 39-066-791-700

➤ It's hard not to love Caffè Greco. The historic coffee house is the oldest in Rome, and having a chance to sip your coffee exactly where Byron and Goethe did is a trip. A pricey trip, but worth it.

Prettiest (and Best) Cappuccino

Er Baretto, Via del Boschetto 132,
39-06-686-4816

➤ If you like your cappuccino pretty, then the cozy, warm, and friendly Er Baretto is the place. An artist when it comes to decorating the richly foamed cappuccini, the

owner prides himself in providing high quality with an almost kitschy attention to flourish.

recipes

caffè shakerato

Serves 1

Once the real Roman heat hits in the summer, the last thing I want is hot coffee. Don't get me wrong. I still need my caffeine more than ever. But the hot part—and even the milk part—is just too much when the thermometer nears 100°F.

My go-to treat is of course a granita di caffè. But it *is* a treat; more of a dessert than a post-meal pick-me-up. So my daily post-lunch hit becomes a caffè shakerato. I'm not sure when this drink started turning up in Italian bars. I suspect it migrated from Greece, where Nescafé is added to ice and water and then shaken to create a luscious and sweet version of iced coffee.

The Italian shakerato is a much more minimal and intense affair. A freshly pulled espresso, poured in a cocktail shaker with a bit of sugar. Abundant ice, a thirty-second hard shake. and then poured ever so elegantly into a stemmed glass—perfect!

A shakerato is always served in a stemmed glass. A champagne flute will do, but I also love to use a martini glass. All very elegant, very cool, and enough caffeine to get me through the few hours left to a sultry Roman workday.

1 demitasse cup freshly brewed espresso
½ to 1 teaspoon sugar
Ice

It's best to shake 1 cup at a time, so things don't get too watered down from the ice melting in the warm coffee.

Brew the espresso, using your favorite home method, and measure out 1 small cup (about ¼ cup).

While still hot, add the sugar and stir to dissolve. Keep stirring so that the coffee cools off a bit. Note that the sugar actually plays a role here not only in sweetening the drink, but also in creating a creamy foam.

Pour into a shaker and add LOTS of ice. Close and shake vigorously for 30 seconds.

Strain into a chilled, stemmed glass. I like a martini glass, but a flute works well, too.

iced coffee with almond milk

Serves 1

I'm a big lover of anything coffee. I love it hot and I love it cold. And as soon as summer begins, I start making daily pilgrimages to Tazza d'Oro for granita di caffè or Fiocco di Neve for caffè affogato con zabaione.

Usually, however, I am limited by the fact that I have to leave the house to grab one of these treats. But recently I realized something very dangerous. After a quick trip to the supermarket down the road, I was able make an addictive caffeinated treat in the comfort of my home way too easily.

Latte di Mandorla is a southern Italian drink that traditionally is made by chopping up fresh almonds, letting them sit in water and sugar overnight, then squeezing the juices through a piece of muslin until you get an ambrosial, milky white almond drink. But nowadays things have, of course, gotten much easier. Latte di Mandorla, or "almond milk," comes premade in a milk carton, available at your local store. My favorite choice is

the extremely unhealthy, overly sugared variety.

So during these hot days of summer, my 11:00 a.m. coffee break consists of iced almond coffee. It's what my sister Robin refers to as a novelty coffee drink. And yes, it's a bit "Starbuckish." But that's OK with me.

> ½ **cup freshly brewed espresso**
> ½ **cup sweetened almond milk (not the healthy no-sugar kind)**
> **Ice**

I like my iced coffee strong, so I brew a pot of espresso. I let it cool off for about 15 minutes, and then add the cold milk.

Fill the glass with as much ice as will fit. And to get the full, almost milk shake–like effect, you really need to use a straw. Trust me.

the leaning tower of artichokes

've loved artichokes for as long as I can remember. In the '60s, growing up in the Midwest, every time we had artichokes it was a pretty big deal. My mother would buy one for each of us, carefully trim away the spiky ends of the leaves, and then plunge them into a big pot of boiling water.

In the meantime, she would unwrap a stick or two of butter and melt it in a small pot on the stovetop. If it was just an ordinary artichoke night, she'd squeeze lemon juice right into the pot. If she was feeling a bit more indulgent, out would come the eggs, and she would whip up her blender hollandaise following the much-stained pages of *Joy of Cooking*.

My sisters and I were passionate about the entire artichoke experience. Watching my mother prepare them was only half of it. Once they got to the table, the true ritual began: carefully taking off each petal, dipping it in the buttery sauce, and then scraping it off with our teeth. Although we weren't as fancy as my grandmother (who had a special set of artichoke dishes with a ridged stand in the middle and a built-in bowl for the butter), my mother did give each of us our own little saucer for dipping.

Once we had worked our way through the leaves, we took up our spoons and learned how to scoop away the furry choke to reveal the meaty heart. After they were cut into chunks, we usually just dumped them into our bowls of butter to make sure they were fully coated, and then, if there happened to be any lemony sauce left in our bowls, we used the already scraped leaves to soak up every last bit. Which makes me wonder: Was it the actual taste of artichokes we loved so much? Or was it the chance to indulge in our own private bowl of lemony butter? Because, to tell you the truth, I can't really remember the actual taste of the artichokes themselves. And, frankly, I can't imagine that they had much taste since they were shipped in from California in what must have been huge refrigerated trucks.

When we moved to Italy not only did my parents attempt to learn the language, they also took cooking lessons. While my sisters and I went off to school my parents learned to conjugate verbs (badly) and whip up *ragù* (much more successfully). I distinctly remember being hugely impressed not only by *fettuccine Bolognese* and *bollito misto* but also by simple plates of local vegetables like *agretti* (a grasslike green) and arugula salad (way before this made its American debut). I also remember the disasters: The night my mother decided to make pizza and we all ended up going out for pizza. (I guess she hadn't learned the word for yeast in Italian.) And then there was the whole *carciofi* incident.

My mother decided to try her hand at one of the all-time best dishes ever invented:

carciofi alla giudea, or Jewish artichokes, a specialty of the Roman Jewish community. They must have seemed like a no-brainer for my parents to attempt making them. Not only did we all love artichokes, but we were Jewish and actually living in the Roman Jewish Ghetto! They would practically make themselves.

Although I was only twelve at the time, I do remember the evening involved hot boiling oil, the smell of burning vegetables, and, if I'm not mistaken, tears and frustration. Another night we ended up going out for pizza.

It wasn't until we made it to Piperno, one of the oldest restaurants in the Jewish Ghetto, a few weeks later that I understood what my parents were trying so hard to re-create. As we sat down at our table in the small piazza, I immediately started surveying what other people were eating. Big brown crispy flowers, it looked like to me. Soon enough our own plates came and my father explained that these were actually artichokes. They looked nothing like anything I knew, and while I started to wonder where the butter was, my dad explained that you just eat the whole thing. I guess we must have looked a little dubious, since he went on, "They're like potato chips, but artichokes."

As my sisters and I began to dig in, we soon realized that as much as we loved the whole lemon butter thing, deep-fried was infinitely better.

all about artichokes

A fresh Roman artichoke is a wonderful thing. The first ones to hit the stands—the cimaroli—are big and fat. They are the ones that grow from the main stalk of the artichoke plant, in early spring, pointing straight up. Not only are they incredibly fragrant and large but also amazingly tender, and have practically no choke or tough inner leaves.

In Italy no one would think of boiling or steaming a whole artichoke and doing the teeth-scraping thing. Why? Because most of the artichokes are so tender that a good portion of the leaf can actually be eaten. But to prepare them does take a bit of work, and can be quite fiddly.

Before you begin, fill a big bowl with cold water. Squeeze a half lemon in, and keep the other half handy. Artichokes oxidize quickly, so you have to rub all cut surfaces with a lemon to prevent this. Once you are finished, you will place the cleaned artichokes in the water until you are ready to season them. You'll also notice that your fingers will probably turn brown, too. Either wear thin gloves (which I hate) or else keep rinsing and rubbing lemon on your hands, especially the fingertips.

Break off the tough, outer leaves of the artichoke until you get down to the leaves that are tender. You'll know you're getting to the tender part by the color. They are usually yellow on the bottom third and pale

violet at the top. When you break off the leaves, do your best to leave on as much of the root of the leaf as possible.

Once you have taken off the tough outer leaves, using a small knife, gently trim away the bright green parts from the stem end. Don't cut off too much, just the green part. This part is quite bitter. Immediately rub the cut parts with a lemon half.

Turn the artichoke on its side, and cut off the top third (the pointy end of the artichoke). Make sure your knife is really sharp. Immediately rub the cut part with lemon, and put the artichoke in water into which you've squeezed a lemon.

If you're lucky, and using the first artichokes of the season, then there shouldn't be much choke. If, however, it's later in the season, then you'll have to use a sharp knife to dig down to get as much of the choke out

as possible. If you are using the artichokes in a dish where they will be cut up, then simply slice them in quarters, lengthwise, and trim out the choke. Just make sure you put the slices back into the lemon water to keep them bright.

monuments to artichokes

If you follow me on social media, then you already know I've got a bit of a love thing going on with artichokes. I buy them, I cook them, I eat them, but, perhaps most of all, I photograph them. I've even invented my own hash tag #carciofogram, so that it's easier than ever to play tag and look at one another's artichokes.

One of my favorite subjects are two monuments to the Roman artichoke. They are not permanent monuments made of marble or bronze, but are built out of the very thing they celebrate. Yes, I'm talking about the Leaning Tower of Artichokes and the Great Wall of Carciofi.

One of the oldest restaurants in the Jewish Ghetto is Giggetto, and its chefs are justly famous for their skill at preparing carciofi alla giudea. During high season they serve more than five hundred a day. Every morning, crates of carciofi are delivered, and retired waiters come in for part-time work to sit in the front of the restaurant and prepare mountains of the globes for their bath in the fryer.

During the first couple of weeks when artichoke season is just starting and the first cimaroli appear—they have huge heads and extra-long stalks—somehow Giggetto manages to tie them together into an eight-foot-tall artichoke tower. For real.

Equally impressive is one of my favorite stands in Campo de' Fiori. Located on the western side of the piazza, in front of the Norcineria Viola, the stand is one of the biggest sellers of carciofi in the market. Piles and piles of the globes pass through it and, for a few brief days, they form a solid four-foot tall, ten-foot-wide wall of purple and green.

when in rome . . .
how to eat artichokes

- Artichokes are best eaten in season, which lasts from April through May. Some restaurants stretch out the season with early artichokes from the south of Italy and late ones from France.

- Fried artichokes: These are best eaten in restaurants that make a LOT of them, all in the Jewish Ghetto. See below for my favorite spots.

- Carciofi alla giudea (deep-fried artichokes) are usually eaten as an antipasto. Carciofi alla romana (Roman-style braised artichokes) are usually eaten as a side dish.

carciofi alla romana

Serves 4

- 4 large artichokes
- 1 bunch fresh flat-leaf parsley
- 3 garlic cloves
- 1 bunch fresh mint
- ½ teaspoon salt
- ¼ teaspoon freshly ground black pepper
- ¼ cup extra-virgin olive oil, plus more as needed for drizzling

Trim the artichokes (see "All About Artichokes," page 55).

Using either a knife or a food processor, chop the parsley, garlic, and mint. As you chop, add ½ teaspoon of salt and about a ¼ teaspoon of pepper. Place in a small bowl and slowly add the ¼ cup of olive oil and stir to amalgamate the mixture.

Lift an artichoke out of the water and gently blot off the water with a paper towel. Hold the artichoke with one hand, and carefully loosen the leaves, being careful not to break any off.

Take a bit the herb mixture and force it in between the leaves and into the center of the artichoke. Keep doing this, until the artichoke is well seasoned. You want to use about 2 tablespoons of mixture per artichoke. Repeat for all the artichokes.

Choose a pot in which the artichokes will fit very snugly, and place them, one against the other, with the tops up. If the stalks of the artichokes are big and thick, you can use those (trimmed of the tough outer part) to keep the artichokes from tipping over. Otherwise, you can use pieces of potato as wedges.

Pour in enough water to come up about 1 inch from the bottom of the pan. Be careful not to pour the water directly onto the artichokes; you don't want to dilute the seasoning. Sprinkle with salt and pepper, and drizzle abundantly with olive oil. Place the lid on the pot and bring to a low simmer. Cook until the artichokes are done, 45 minutes to an hour. You can check to see if they are done by pulling on a leaf. It should come out easily. Also, check the water frequently as the artichokes cook to make sure it hasn't boiled away, adding more if needed.

Carciofi alla romana are best served at room temperature. I like to place them in a deep serving dish, with the cooking liquid at the bottom, and accompany them with lots of fresh bread to soak it up.

pasta with artichokes, peas, and mint pesto

Serves 6

When it's artichoke season, I buy, cook, and eat as many artichokes as possible. It's also when it becomes difficult for me to take photographs of anything *but*

(continued)

artichokes. I pass by that monument to carciofi love, the leaning tower of Giggetto almost every day. Then there's the market, where at least four different varieties of purple and green globes vie for my attention.

As photogenic as these beauties are while posing in all their pristine glory, they pretty much turn into an army-green, dull mush when cooked. I'm not talking about the crispy fried carciofi alla giudea, which have their own golden charm, but about almost any other dish in which artichokes figure as a main ingredient. Pasta, risotto, stews . . . it's not easy to capture a photograph nearing anything as gorgeous as they actually taste.

After a recent trip to Bari, Domenico came home with a bag of handmade *strascinati*. Stascinati are a cousin of orecchiette. They are usually made with *semola di grano duro*, a type of coarsely ground durum wheat flour and water (no eggs). The small bits of dough are artfully dragged across a rough wooden board to form their shape. While orecchiette involves the expert use of a thumb to form an ear-shaped little bite, strascinati need three fingers to pull the strip of dough into a 2-inch oblong form. But these particular strascinati were even more special. They had been made with the addition of *farina di gran'arso*, a type of burned flour that gives the pasta not only a hauntingly toasted taste, but also, as an added bonus, a not-so-attractive gray color.

OK, maybe I'm exaggerating just a little. But let me digress a bit and tell you how I come up with my blog posts. I don't have any big weeklong or monthlong plan regarding what I'm going to be writing about. Instead, I usually go to the farmers' market on Saturday and then, as I'm putting away my produce, I take the time to photograph the ingredients before I put them in the fridge. I do this because (a) the vegetables are looking their best, and (b) the light is great at that time of day.

Then I go about my week, cooking up what I've bought. I don't decide to cook something specifically for the blog; instead, what I cook just turns up there. But this is where the photography part gets tricky. We eat dinner at 8:00 p.m., and there is very little natural light. So I try to keep something aside to photograph the next day, when the light is better.

This game plan usually works out just fine. Except, of course, when what I'm about to photograph is a big bowl of gray pasta dressed with an army-green mixture of artichokes and peas. And no amount of midday sun or bright-tasting ingredients—like lemon zest from Ravello and freshly picked mint from the terrace— can change that. A brilliantly glazed ceramic plate from Vietri does, however, do wonders.

Despite the dullness of the colors though, this dish really does scream spring, and brings out the best of the beautiful artichokes. The sauce is mostly trimmed artichokes with a good amount of freshly shelled peas. To pull it all together I use a mint pesto, made with almonds and heaping quantities of grated zest from the untreated lemons Domenico brings home from Ravello.

I could have used a prettier pasta in this dish, I guess, and you are welcome to do so. And I meant to add a few barely cooked, bright green peas at the end, but I didn't. So while this dish doesn't win any awards for beauty, I think it does win the best-taste award for Miss Springtime Pasta of March.

6 large artichokes

Zest and 1 tablespoon juice from 1 large untreated lemon

3 tablespoons and ⅓ cup extra-virgin olive oil, plus more as needed

1 small onion, chopped

1¼ teaspoons salt, plus more as needed

½ cup water, plus more as needed

2 cups fresh shelled peas

1 big bunch fresh mint (about 1½ cups mint leaves)

2 garlic cloves

¼ cup almonds

¼ to ⅓ cup grated mild pecorino or Parmesan cheese

1 pound (500 grams) strascinati pasta, or pasta of your choice

Freshly ground black pepper

Trim the artichokes by removing the outer tough leaves and the sharp tips. Cut away any bright green bits until you get to the soft heart. Slice thinly and put in a bowl of water to which you've added about a tablespoon of fresh lemon juice.

In a large sauté pan over medium heat, warm the 3 tablespoons of olive oil. Add the onion and 1 teaspoon of the salt, and cook until the onion has softened but not browned, about 8 minutes.

Drain the artichoke slices and add to the pan, stir, and add about ½ cup of water. Simmer until softened, but not browned, adding a bit more water if needed.

When the artichokes are almost done, add the peas, and cook until tender. Taste and adjust with more salt if needed, but remember the pesto will also add flavor.

Put the mint, garlic, almonds, lemon zest, and remaining ¼ teaspoon salt in a small food processor and puree until smooth. (You may have to add a bit of olive oil to make it blend.) Then add all of the ⅓ cup of olive oil until the mixture is well chopped and combined.

Transfer the pesto to a small bowl and add the grated cheese.

Bring a large pot of salted water to a boil. Add the pasta and cook until al dente.

Meanwhile, check the artichoke mixture and reheat if it has gotten cold.

Drain the pasta, reserving 1 cup of the pasta cooking water. Transfer the pasta to a large bowl and toss with the artichoke mixture.

(continued)

If the pesto seems very thick, add a ladleful of the reserved pasta cooking water to thin it out a bit, and then add to the pasta, tossing to mix it well. At this point, you can also add a bit more of the reserved cooking water to loosen things up and make it a bit creamier if desired.

Serve topped with freshly ground black pepper.

artichoke lasagna

Serves 8

Easter in Italy is pretty predictable foodwise. Like most good Italians, I almost always cook lamb. You'd think that after years of cooking the same cut of meat I'd get adventurous in the recipe department. But even though I toy around with the idea of delving into Wolfert or Bittman for something a bit—I don't know—Middle Eastern? I always go back to the same old, same old. Antipasto for the Easter meal is also carved in stone. Domenico is from Bari and so we always have *sopressata*, which his mother brings up in her suitcase from Puglia. Then there are hard-boiled eggs, which we eat cut in chunks and drizzle with olive oil. A jumble of fresh fava beans and a hunk of pecorino completes that course. Dessert? *Pastiera*. Is there anything else? But the first course, that's another thing. At least here I feel free to change year to year. One year it might be

asparagus soup, another *pasta al forno*. More often than not artichokes figure, since they're spring defined. One of my favorites is *lasagna ai carciofi,* which I keep as simple as possible—mostly artichokes, with just three layers of pasta and enough *besciamella* to hold it all together, and handfuls of grated Parmigiano-Reggiano and pecorino (that goes without saying).

I know that making and using fresh sheets of lasagna is probably a whole lot better. But I love the dried ones that you don't even have to cook. I even think that they give a lighter texture, which I like, especially when making a dish that is rich in butter and milk. And speaking of besciamella, you'll notice I substitute chicken broth for almost half of the milk. That's my attempt at making it a tad less heavy.

Also, I know some people love to add on the layers with lasagna. But I think you should never ever have more than three layers of noodles, otherwise it just turns into a solid brick.

Lasagna
- 10 large artichokes
- Juice of 1 lemon
- 1 tablespoon unsalted butter
- 1 tablespoon extra-virgin olive oil
- 1 onion, chopped
- 1 tablespoon fresh thyme leaves
- Salt
- Freshly ground black pepper

½ cup (120 milliliters) water

1 cup (250 milliliters) dry white wine

1 pound (500 grams) no-boil lasagna
noodles

1½ cups grated Parmesan cheese

3 tablespoons grated pecorino cheese

Besciamella

3 cups (¾ liter) chicken broth

4 cups (1 liter) whole milk

7 tablespoons (100 grams) unsalted
butter

1 cup (100 grams) all-purpose flour

Clean the artichokes, trimming off the outer leaves and cutting out the inner choke. Cut them into eighths and let them soak in a bowl of water with lemon juice until ready to use. (See "All About Artichokes," page 55.)

In a pan large enough to hold all of the artichokes, melt the butter with the olive oil. Add the onion and thyme, and season with salt and pepper. Cook over low heat until the onion has softened. Add the drained and dried artichokes and stir in the water. Cover the pan and let the artichokes cook for about 8 minutes or so, with the lid on. Lift the lid and stir them; they should be getting pretty soft. Add the wine and let it boil away. Continue to cook the artichokes until very tender, but not falling apart, adding a bit more water if needed. Turn off heat.

To make the besciamella, mix the broth and milk and heat gently. Put the butter

in a pot large enough to hold the milk and broth. Let melt and then slowly add the flour, stirring all the time; it will get quite thick. Once you have added all the flour, keep stirring, over low heat, for a couple of more minutes.

Slowly add the hot milk and broth, stirring with a whisk or wooden spoon; it will look clumpy at first but will eventually thin out. Once you have added all the liquid, keep stirring over low heat until the besciamella is the consistency of crepe batter. You want it kind of "liquidy," since you're using dried noodles.

Now you're ready to assemble the lasagna. Preheat the oven to 350°F (180°C). Choose a large roasting pan, about 13 x 16 inches, and butter or oil it.

Using a ladle, fill the bottom with enough of the besciamella to cover it completely, about ⅛ inch. Lay dried noodles on top of this, side by side, to form the first layer. Ladle some more besciamella on top, covering the noodles. Then add half of the artichokes, spreading them out evenly. Sprinkle with ½ cup of the grated Parmesan, 1 tablespoon of the pecorino, and some salt and pepper.

Repeat with another layer: noodles, besciamella, artichokes, cheese, salt, and pepper.

Lay a final layer of noodles on top, cover generously with besciamella (you should be almost to the bottom of the pot), pouring some more in the sides

(continued)

and making sure you cover every square inch of the dried noodles. Finish with the remaining cheese.

Bake in the preheated oven for 25 minutes, or until the lasagna is bubbly and the top is nicely browned.

Let rest about 10 minutes before cutting and serving. It's even better if you let it cool completely, even in the fridge, and reheat later that day or the next.

risotto with artichokes

Serves 4 to 6

One of my favorite ways to eat artichokes is in risotto. I have to admit I don't make risotto so often. Partly out of laziness, but also because for years Sophie decided she didn't like risotto. (She's a pasta girl, 100 percent—so Roman it's hard to believe.) But once Sophie went off to university the risotto door swung wide open.

There are certainly risottos that are prettier, but artichoke risotto is one of my favorites. There is something about the creaminess of the starchy rice that blends so well with the sweet but bitter flavor of the artichokes.

There are plenty of artichoke risotto recipes out there. But I add a few twists to mine that I think make it even better. Rather than use onions, I opt for end-of-winter leeks. They are milder than onions,

and besides adding a sweeter allium taste, they also dissolve and add to the overall creaminess. And while wild *mentuccia* (*calamintha nepeta L.*) is called for in a lot of artichoke dishes in Rome, I prefer *menta romana* (*mentha spicata L.*), which I add at the very end, along with freshly cut strips of lemon peel.

These last two additions not only contribute a springy freshness to the dish but also give it a much-needed burst of color—because, come on, *risotto ai carciofi* isn't going to win any beauty contests, even if I do put it on a bright blue plate.

Let me say right here that when I make risotto, I usually err on the side of whatever vegetable I'm using. In other words, my ratio of vegetables to rice leans more on the vegetable side than is traditional.

And yes, you do need all the butter. Believe me.

6 cups broth (1½ liters) (best if homemade, but if in a pinch, use prepared)

4 tablespoons (½ stick/60 grams) unsalted butter

1 tablespoon extra-virgin olive oil

2 large leeks, washed of grit and sliced

Salt

Freshly ground black pepper

6 large artichokes, cleaned and sliced (see "All About Artichokes," page 55)

10 ounces (300 grams) arborio rice

½ cup (100 milliliters) dry white wine
½ cup grated Parmigiano-Reggiano
   cheese (although I have used grated
   local pecorino instead)
⅓ cup fresh mint leaves, torn
Grated zest of 1 lemon

In a large pot, bring the broth to a slow simmer. In a separate large pot, add 2 tablespoons of the butter and the olive oil. Heat gently, add the leeks, and season with salt and pepper. Cook for about 8 minutes, or until the leeks are wilted.

Add the cut-up artichokes, stir, and cook until they become tender, about 10 minutes or so. If they start to brown, add a bit of water.

Add the rice and stir well, letting the rice absorb any liquid that is in the pan. Add the wine and cook until absorbed. Add about 2 cups of the broth, stir, and let simmer. Keep adding broth, a ladleful at a time, until the rice is just about done. This will take anywhere from 15 to 20 minutes, depending on the rice.

When the rice is about 4 minutes from being done (it will be still a bit firm to the tooth), add the rest of the butter and give a good stir. Continue cooking for about 3 more minutes, then add the cheese, stir, and remove from the heat.

Let the rice sit for a couple of minutes. Add half the mint and lemon, and stir to combine. Spoon the risotto onto individual plates and top each dish with a bit of mint and lemon zest. Serve a bowl of grated cheese on the table for sprinkling.

chicken livers and artichokes

Serves 2 to 4

One of my favorite springtime dishes is *coratella con carciofi*. This seasonal dish combines not only spring artichokes but also the liver, lungs, and heart of spring lamb. This is something I make whenever I can find *coratella*, which I admit isn't easy. Not all butchers carry it, and since it's only available for a few short months a year (when the lambs are young) that makes it even harder. And I imagine if it's hard for me to find coratella here in Rome, it's almost impossible where you are.

So I'm sharing my backup version: chicken livers with artichokes. I love chicken livers but cut down my consumption of them when I became suspicious of where those livers were coming from. I have long since stopped buying chicken at the supermarket, or from any butcher I don't know very well. The problem was that my organic source was always limited, and almost never had livers.

All that changed with the opening of the farmers' market here in Rome. Not

(continued)

only does my farmer bring in delicious, homegrown, organic chickens, but she also always has packs of chicken livers, which, evidently, no one else seems to want. When faced with the choice of buying a pack of chicken parts for 18 euros or a pack of chicken livers for 4 euros, I'm going to choose the livers every time. Really, she almost gives them to me for free.

I had the idea of combining them with artichokes last week, as the livers I buy are almost like coratella, since they have the hearts attached as well.

Actually, if you want to know the truth, lately I've been combining artichokes with just about everything. Because, well, who can resist?

> 6 to 8 artichokes
> 2 tablespoons extra-virgin olive oil
> 1 medium onion
> Salt
> Freshly ground black pepper
> ½ cup water
> 1 pound chicken livers
> 1 cup dry white wine
> A squeeze of fresh lemon juice

Trim the artichokes by removing the tough outer leaves and sharp tips. Slice into ½-inch wedges. (See "All About Artichokes," page 55.)

Pour the olive oil into a pan large enough to hold everything and place over medium heat. Add the onion, salt, and pepper and cook until the onion has softened but not browned, about 10 minutes.

Add the artichokes, stir, and add the water. Cook, stirring, until the artichokes start to become tender, about 10 minutes.

In the meantime, trim the chicken livers of any extra fat. You may also need to separate them if there is a membrane connecting the two halves. If the heart is included, trim this of extra fat and cut in half.

Add the livers and heart to the artichokes and stir. Cook over medium heat until the livers start to brown. Add a bit more salt and the white wine and continue to cook until done. The livers should lose any shade of pinkness when cut in half. Taste for salt and pepper and adjust if needed.

Just before serving, squeeze a bit of lemon juice on top and mix through.

Although I consider this a main dish, I think that if you chopped the livers and the artichokes a bit smaller, it would work equally well atop toasted bread as an antipasto.

raw artichoke salad

Serves 1

Artichokes are fiddly. Before you get to the deliciousness you have to deal with a lot of heavy armor, tearing, trimming, and cutting your way past the green and purple leaves to the pale yellow heart. I tend to forget this part of the equation when I am loading up at the market. When I blithely say to the vendor, "Give me eight—no, twelve!—artichokes, please," I don't actually picture myself sitting down to trim them all. Sometimes, rather than deal with my artichoke-filled fridge all at once, I take things one carciofo at a time. Because during high season, when each artichoke is as big as baby's head, it takes just one huge fat globe to turn into my lunch.

First I trim it of its outer leaves, then slice the heart paper thin. Spread it on a plate with a crumble of sheep's milk cheese on top, then all it takes is a swirl of olive oil to bring it to perfection. And that is lunch, as long as artichoke season lasts.

1 large artichoke, trimmed and cut into
    thin slices (see "All About Artichokes,"
    page 55)
Fresh lemon juice
Crumbly semi-fresh pecorino or
    Parmesan cheese
Extra-virgin olive oil (or, if you can get it,
    Colonna Granverde), for drizzling
Sea salt
Freshly ground black pepper

Once you've trimmed your artichoke as described earlier, cut it into paper-thin slices and lay it on a plate. Quickly squeeze fresh lemon juice over it and toss, so it doesn't oxidize and turn brown. Crumble some cheese on top, drizzle with olive oil, and sprinkle with salt and pepper.

{ **chapter 8** }

"mi piace la cicoria!"

the roman passion for vegetables

understand that when kids come home from college they expect to find their favorite comfort foods. Meat loaf and mashed potatoes maybe? In Italy it's more likely to be
nonna's pasta al forno. But my daughter? Want to know what Sophie craves when she
has been away from home for too long? *Cicoria.* Yes, chicory. All she dreams about when
coming back home is a big platter of bitter greens.

Sophie started out like any normal child, refusing to eat vegetables for quite a long time.
She was always partial to savory, salty, and sour and so loved anything that was cheesy or
cured or that she could squeeze lemon juice over. Tripe and prosciutto were favorites. Peas
and carrots, not so much.

All that changed when she was about thirteen years old, and somehow "discovered"
cucumbers. I think when she realized that she could take cucumbers and turn them into a
briny Greek salad, full of olives and feta cheese, it sort of opened up the floodgates.

Her chicory epiphany came at the takeout counter of Roscioli. One of the most famous bakeries in Rome, it has expanded to include a *tavola calda*, where prepared food
is sold cafeteria-style. Sophie would meet my husband, Domenico, there for lunch, and
somehow "discovered" cicoria. No wonder she liked it. Even though this is the bitterest of

greens, Roscioli softened the blow by first boiling it, then sautéing it in a massive dose of olive oil with liberal amounts of garlic, red pepper, and salt. And then some more salt.

I shouldn't have been surprised by Sophie's eventual obsession with the most typical of Roman vegetables. Even if she is 50 percent American, her tastes in almost everything run 100 percent Roman. While her enthusiasm for Roma, the local football team, has waned over the years (at least she doesn't wear that orange and maroon fan scarf all the time), her passion for Roman vegetables has only increased.

And Romans do love their vegetables, eating them at almost every meal, which is why I was so puzzled by a question that I often get from visitors to Rome: Why don't Italians eat vegetables? And, if you look at almost any menu in any Italian restaurant (which is what these tourists are doing), you would indeed come away with the idea that vegetables are not part of the meal. There is a section for *antipasti* (appetizers), then *primi* (pasta and soups), and *secondi* (main courses). But tucked in between *secondi* and *dolce* (desserts) is a one-line section that most tourists just skip over: *contorni*.

Contorni translates as "surrounding" and these dishes are meant to surround or frame the main dish. The only problem is that nine times out of ten this section is left completely blank. So even if you could recognize the Italian words for spinach (*spinaci*), zucchini (*zucchini*), and peppers

(*pepperoni*), you would almost never see them printed here in black and white.

This is not because Romans don't care about vegetables. It is because they care too much. Romans eat seasonally, and are completely and utterly passionate about certain vegetables. Nowhere is this more evident than on simple restaurant menus. While the primi and secondi are usually pretty stable, rounded out by daily and seasonal specialties, when it comes to vegetables and side dishes it's a completely different story. Many of these *trattorie* shop weekly or even daily. And if you can be sure to always find the ingredients for *bucatini all'amatriciana* and *saltimbocca alla romana*, artichokes, fava beans, and broccoli rabe are still strictly tied to the seasons.

That blank space on the menu doesn't mean the restaurant doesn't have any side dishes. Every Roman knows to ask. It's the waiter who will fill in the blanks, telling you the *contorno* of the day. And unlike in the States, where a main course is served with a side dish, Romans consider the side dish to be so important an element to the meal that it is ordered separately.

And as if that weren't complicated enough, there is a slight distinction between contorni (side dishes) and *verdure* (vegetables). For instance, if you ask what contorni are available that evening, you might hear about potatoes, chicory, and salad. But somehow, those stuffed zucchini that you saw on a plate heading to the table next to you would not be included in this list because they are stuffed and so considered either an antipasto or a main dish.

ordering salad

There may be nothing that confuses an Italian waiter more than an American asking for a salad at the start of a meal. It's almost as bad as ordering a cappuccino after dinner, but not quite. Domenico remembers being thoroughly confused when he arrived in Kansas as a student and his first meal started out with a plateful of lettuce. He thought that was it, the end of the meal before it had even begun, because in Italy, salad is always served after the main course.

Why? I've never really thought about it and the only reason I can give you is that once again, at the table, Italians are concerned with digestion. My mother-in-law would never think of ending a meal without a piece of fruit *per digerire* (to help digest), and I think the idea of a leafy salad at the end of a heavy meal must play the same role roughagewise.

Traditionally, when it comes to ordering a salad in an Italian restaurant you can have *verde* (green) or *misto* (mixed). Take my advice and please just order the green salad. *Insalata misto* has evolved, in the Rome restaurant scene, to mean a plateful of perfectly good greens topped by some insipid grated carrot (which no Roman would ever eat at home) and a few out-of-season cherry tomatoes. The only exception to this rule would be if it is indeed summer and arugula and tomatoes are actually in season. Then by all means order this.

puntarelle

The most famous of Roman salads is, of course, the exception to any rule. If you've had *puntarelle,* then you are probably swooning by now (it's a love kind of thing). If you haven't, then let me introduce you. Puntarelle is a type of chicory. When you examine a head of puntarelle, it looks green and leafy—at least at first glance. But start to pry apart the outer leaves and you'll soon find the pale green, crunchy center that sets this vegetable apart. The core of the vegetable grows into multiple pointy spears that are almost asparagus-like at the tips.

The taste is slightly bitter, with loads of crunch. In the winter, when it comes into season and is dressed with a lemony garlic vinaigrette, it's what your sluggish body has been asking for, but didn't realize. When I've tired of roasted root vegetables and every kind of boiled green, puntarelle is the fresh crunch I crave.

Puntarelle is like many of life's pleasures—a pain to prep. First you must peel off the outer dark green leaves. Then each spear must be cut off the central core. And finally, each tiny spear has to be cut, lengthwise, into thin strips. The strips are then put into water, to remove some of their bitterness, and also to make them curl up.

Luckily, as with all fussy vegetables, in Rome you can buy them prepared and ready to go at most markets.

Back in the olden days (like ten years ago) the vendors in Campo de' Fiori would use a small sharp knife to carefully cut the spears into strips. But then, all of a sudden, a clever puntarelle cutter started showing up. I assumed each vendor made their own, but it turns out it was one housewares guy who specialized in them. (It's the stand across from the flower vendors.) He's even patented the thing, and has a website, www.puntarelle.it.

The cutter is genius. A series of stainless steel wires is stretched across a small wooden frame, crossing to make a grid. The vegetable vendor then takes each puntarelle tip, and forces it through, before throwing it in its water bath to soak.

roman vegetables: when and how

If you're in Rome, there are certain vegetables you should seek out. Many have a short season, so don't be disappointed if you miss them, since it's just another reason to come back.

Artichokes

Carciofo romanesco: The big fat artichokes from the area outside of Rome, near Cerveteri and Ladispoli. The first artichokes to appear come from the top of the plant and are called cimaroli or *mammole*. These are especially tender, and have almost no choke. The fat stalks, once trimmed, are also edible.

Season: February to May.

Dishes: carciofi alla giudea (deep-fried Roman artichokes); carciofi alla romana (Roman-style braised artichokes stuffed with wild mint and garlic).

Where: I've never had a good carciofi alla giudea outside of the Jewish Ghetto in Rome. My three sources are Giggetto, Piperno, and Sora Margherita. I particularly like the extra-crispy ones served at Sora Margherita. They are at their best during the late winter and spring, when Roman artichokes are in season, but all three of these restaurants offer them all year long, using artichokes imported from Sicily, Sardegna, and France.

Puntarelle

A variety of chicory whose crisp hearts are cut into curly strips and then dressed in an anchovy and garlic vinaigrette.

Season: Late fall to winter.

Where: Almost every restaurant will be serving puntarelle in season, although you will almost never see it on the menu. Make sure you ask.

Zucchini Romanesco

This type of zucchini differentiates itself from other types by its slightly curved form and highly ridged surface. It has a very strong flavor, and its low water content means that it never becomes mushy and soft, like the dark green smooth variety.

Season: The traditional season is from May through September, since this is a summer vegetable. These days though, many local growers use hothouses to extend the season almost all year long.

Dishes: *concia di zucchini* (fried, marinated zucchini); *zucchini ripieni* (stuffed zucchini); *zucchini fritti* (fried zucchini).

Where: Sora Margherita, Piazza delle Cinque Scole 30, 39-06-687-4216.

Although concia di zucchini is a simple dish, it's hard to find in Rome. Sora Margherita makes it almost every day when zucchini are in season. Its version is quite spicy, and browned to a crisp.

Broccolo Romanesco

This bright green vegetable is a relative of cauliflower but the florets are formed in a geometric whirling pattern that gives it an almost outer space–like appearance. The strong color is matched by an even stronger taste that is somewhat of a mix between broccoli and cauliflower.

Season: November to March.

Dishes: *minestra di pasta, broccoli e arzilla* (pasta and broccoli in ray fish broth). A very old-fashioned Roman recipe that is almost impossible to find these days.

Where: Armando al Pantheon, Salita dei Crescenzi 31, 39-06-6880-3034.

While it is very difficult to find in Rome, your best bet is at Armando, where the menu changes daily. You can call ahead and ask if it is being served.

when in rome . . . eating vegetables in restaurants

- Main courses do not automatically come with a side dish; you must order it.

- Vegetables are usually listed on a menu as contorni, or "side dishes."

- In addition to the listed vegetables, always ask for daily specials for contorni, which change seasonally.

- In a restaurant, I often order a plate of vegetables as one of my courses. For instance, after a plate of pasta, I'll just have an order of spinach or some artichokes as my secondo.

recipes

verdure ripassata

Serves 4

Throughout the fall and winter and into spring, the Roman markets are full of piles of chicory, Swiss chard, and flowering broccoli. They are so ubiquitous that they often don't even appear on restaurant menus. Yet if you ask, you will be told: Yes, we have chicory (or Swiss chard, or *broccoletti*). The

(continued)

choice then is between *all'agro* (simply boiled, then dressed with olive oil and lemon juice) or *ripassata in padella* (sautéed in the pan).

Of course, ripassata is the way to go. Boiled greens of any sort are drained, then sautéed in a pan with olive oil, garlic, and hot red pepper flakes.

> 2 pounds (1 kilo) chicory, Swiss chard, or broccoli rabe
> 1 tablespoon kosher salt, for boiling greens, plus more as needed
> 3 tablespoons extra-virgin olive oil
> 3 garlic cloves, chopped
> 1 teaspoon hot red pepper flakes

Wash the greens well, and remove any tough stems.

Bring a large pot of water to a boil and add the salt. Add the greens and cook until done. For spring chicory this shouldn't take long; maybe 8 minutes or so. If you're unsure, take out a piece and taste it. The stalks should be quite tender. Adjust for other types of vegetables, but you do want them well done, not just wilted. Drain the greens.

In a large frying pan, heat the olive oil and add the garlic and red pepper flakes. When the garlic starts to become fragrant, after about 3 minutes, add the drained chicory. Toss very well, so that the chicory is completely coated with the seasoned oil. Taste and correct for salt. Serve hot or at room temperature.

concia di zucchini

Serves 4

One of my favorite ways to eat zucchini, especially when they are small, tender, and firm, is *alla concia.* This is an old Roman Jewish recipe that combines tender zucchini with the strong tastes of vinegar and red pepper. Since this is a summer dish, my feeling is that originally the hefty dose of vinegar was a way of keeping the dish from spoiling during the heat. And in fact, most restaurants make it with much more vinegar than I use at home.

If possible, make sure you get hold of *zucchini romanesco* for this dish, since their low water content means that they will caramelize and brown before turning mushy like regular zucchini.

> 2 pounds (1 kilo) small, tender zucchini romanesco
> 4 garlic cloves
> ⅓ cup (230 milliliters) extra-virgin olive oil
> ¼ to ½ teaspoon hot red pepper flakes
> 1 to 2 tablespoons wine vinegar
> Salt
> ¼ cup chopped fresh flat-leaf parsley

Slice the zucchini into very thin rounds.

Peel and lightly crush the garlic cloves with the side of your knife.

Heat the oil in a large frying pan over medium-high heat. Add the garlic and red

(continued)

pepper flakes, and cook until the garlic becomes golden. Gently scoop it up and discard it, leaving the pepper behind.

Add the zucchini slices, and flip them around in the pan until they turn a deep golden brown. You may have to do this in two batches, depending on the size of your pan. You definitely don't want to overcrowd the pan, since you want the zucchini to cook as fast as possible.

Once the zucchini are tender yet still firm, scoop them out and drain them on a paper towel. Then toss them wth the vinegar and salt.

Spread the zucchini out on a platter and top with parsley. This dish is served room temperature. I also often use it as a topping for bruschetta or crostini.

Note: The amount of vinegar depends on how strong your vinegar is and also how vinegary you want the final dish to be. I err on the side of less.

broccolo romanesco and anchovy salad

Serves 4–6

There are some things that I can't get enough of. *Broccolo romanesco* is one of them. This strange-looking, fractile bright green cruciferous vegetable is some sort of mash-up between cauliflower and broccoli. But unlike broccoli, it doesn't have that tendency to go all mushy.

And unlike cauliflower . . . Well, isn't cauliflower just a wee bit boring in its smooth, white look and cabbagey taste?

Another thing I can never get enough of? Really good anchovies. I'm not talking about those wimpy filets that seem to fall apart at the lightest touch and only really taste of salt. I'm talking about big, fat, thick anchovies from Sicily or Spain that have been packed into a jar full of olive oil. Rather than just taste like salt, they are the essence of the briny sea where they come from. Chewy, firm, and meaty, they hold their own in almost any dish, and they always make things better.

This winter salad used lemon to add brightness and couldn't be simpler. The broccolo is briefly steamed, just enough to cook it through. I then make a dressing of olive oil, Meyer lemon juice, grated rind, and enough chopped anchovies to satisfy even *my* absurd attraction to these little fishies.

I toss everything together while the broccolo is still warm, which really gives the anchovies and Meyer lemon a chance to shine. The longer you let it sit, the better it gets. I prefer the dish room temperature, which is why I'm calling it a salad. And if you do put it in the fridge, make sure you let it come back to room temperature before digging in.

1 Meyer lemon
8 big anchovy fillets, untreated
¼ cup fruity extra-virgin olive oil

1 medium head of broccolo romanesco
(see note)
Salt
Freshly ground black pepper

Peel the lemon skin using a vegetable peeler. Make sure not to peel any of the white pith. Chop finely and place in a small bowl.

Chop the anchovy fillets into ¼-inch-sized pieces. Place in the bowl with the lemon peel.

Add the olive oil and the juice from the lemon. Stir. Let sit for at least a half hour but no more than 2 hours, to let the flavors blend.

Divide the broccolo into bite-size florets. Try to keep them intact since they are so great looking. Steam for about 5 minutes.

Place the still-hot broccolo in a wide shallow bowl. Pour the dressing over and toss carefully. Cool to room temperature and serve. Add salt and pepper to taste.

Note: If you can't find broccolo romanesco, you have my permission to use cauliflower.

how to eat pasta like a roman

would love to tell you that my earliest memories of pasta involve a nonna rolling out paper-thin sheets of freshly made dough ready to assemble into a bubbling tray of lasagna for a Sunday lunch. Or that I remember the entire family gathered round the kitchen table, meticulously assembling tiny tortellini for a holiday feast.

Even though I have many delicious memories of food while growing up in St. Louis (barbecue, fried chicken, and even tacos) pasta has absolutely no place. Not only was freshly made pasta off the radar, I don't even remember dried pasta in a box. No, my first forays into pasta were 100 percent typical of a 1960s childhood in suburban St. Louis.

Yes, I'm talking about SpaghettiOs. Pasta in a can. With sauce. Ready to heat up. But don't worry, it's not as if we ate this every day. No. It was saved as a special treat, for my sisters and me to enjoy on the nights my parents went out to dinner. And as a extra-special treat? My mother would splurge and get SpaghettiOs with Meatballs.

We did get to enjoy one other "authentic" pasta every so often: toasted ravioli. Fat meat-filled ravioli that were breaded, then fried and served with a marinara dipping sauce. St. Louis actually had a large Italian community, and there were many restaurants located in the area of town called "The Hill." But if you're thinking deep-fried ravioli doesn't sound very Italian, you're right. It was a St. Louis invention through and through.

All this is to say that when it comes to pasta I had no preconceptions when we arrived in Italy. But the strange thing is that when I began to think of my life-changing childhood pasta memories concerning my family's arrival in Italy when I was twelve, I found I had none. I had vivid memories of things like artichokes, pizza bianca, and veal, but pasta? Nothing. A blank.

But when I say nothing, it's not that we didn't eat pasta. We did. Every day. But there was nothing earth-shattering or life-changing in a way I can describe. One day we were in St. Louis opening a can of SpaghettiOs and the next day we were in Rome digging into heaping bowls of *spaghetti al pomodoro*.

I think this has to do with the fact that we assimilated so quickly and so deeply that almost immediately we were taking pasta for granted. Unlike pizza or gelato, which were still reserved for special treats, pasta was just there, showing up for at least one meal every day. We had become Italian.

The state of Italian cooking in the States has obviously changed since I left St. Louis all those years ago. And even if SpaghettiOs still exist (I follow them on Twitter), most people arriving as visitors to Italy have a pretty good idea of what well-made pasta tastes like. The Food Network, Mario Batali, and Marcella Hazan have taken care of that. And in fact, pasta usually ranks high on their list of things "to do," as in "We are going to see the Col-

osseum, visit the Vatican, and eat pasta." As easy and straightforward as this may sound, I get e-mails and questions almost daily about how people should do this. Where should they eat pasta? What is the best pasta in Rome? What is my favorite pasta?

And then, of course, there are the cooking questions. You'd think that with all the Italian cookbooks and websites out there all the possible questions would have been answered before they were even asked. So here, for the record, are my FAQs for pasta.

pasta: fresh or dried?

I want to admit something that might appear to be somewhat controversial from a writer who prides herself on talking about Italian food. I do not make pasta.

I'm not talking about cooking pasta dishes, which I do all the time. I'm talking about taking flour and eggs, mixing them together, and turning them into miraculously thin fettuccine, plump ravioli, or tiny tortellini. Yes, I've ventured into *gnudi*, gnocchi, and other easy-to-form pastas. But the egg pasta that involves either rolling out a sheet or pushing it through some kind of machine? Almost never.

I say almost never because I have a vague recollection of having made fettuccine one weekend while we were out in Todi, about fifteen years ago. That vague memory of it being hard, messy, and frustrating was, I guess, what has kept my pasta machine on the top shelf of the pantry for more than a decade.

I realize that if I practiced and gave it a go, I could master fresh pasta. I've done so with bread and pizza, which are equally messy and technically challenging endeavors involving flour and water. I've come to the conclusion that part of my resistance to pasta making is that I just don't have to. And this has everything to do with living in Rome.

If I am craving fresh pasta, there are still places where I can buy it. There is a family-run store in my neighborhood that turns out bright yellow sheets of fresh pasta daily, ready to be cut or stuffed into almost any shape I can ask for.

pasta in restaurants: is it handmade?

This is a question that drives me crazy. After someone asks me for a restaurant recommendation, the follow-up question is almost always "Do they make their own pasta?" As if that is the deciding factor of a restaurant's quality. While handmade pasta, made from flour and eggs, is delicious, it isn't always the right pasta for every dish. And in Rome? Most of the iconic pastas call for dried pasta.

Handmade fettuccine is great when you're talking about rich sauces like Bolognese or a meaty ragu from farther north. Those rich sauces, full of luscious butter and fatty meat, pair perfectly with the highly absorbent nature of fettuccine, pappardelle, and tagliatelle. But when we start talking about the minimally beautiful pasta dishes of Rome, like carbonara, *gricia,* and *cacio e pepe,* which have barely any added moisture, the pasta of choice is penne or rigatoni.

why aren't you fat?

You have no idea how often I am asked this question. That, or the other slightly different version "Why aren't Italians fat?" This question comes right on the heels of the question "Do Italians eat pasta every day?" And "How can you eat a first course and a second course?" Yes, we do eat pasta every day. And yes, even I can manage to eat a pasta course followed by a meat course. But the pasta we are all eating comes in a very controlled portion. When it comes to eating pasta, Italians are very measurement conscious. And it's a very easy formula to follow: 100 grams (3½ ounces) or less of pasta per person. It is never a heaping portion like one you would expect in the States.

what pasta should we eat in rome?

These are the pasta dishes you are most likely to run into in almost any restaurant in Rome.

Cacio e Pepe: This is the simplest of Roman pastas, with only three ingredients: pasta, cheese, and black pepper. It is almost always made with dried pasta, and much depends not only on the quality of the ingredients, but on the skill of the cook preparing it. The cheese, Pecorino Romano, needs to coat each piece of pasta, without clumping up at the bottom of the dish. The secret ingredient is the pasta cooking water.

Pasta alla Gricia: For some reason this one falls off most radars. It's like a cacio e pepe with guanciale. Or, if you prefer, carbonara without eggs.

Carbonara: Again, a minimal number of ingredients: pasta, guanciale, cheese, and eggs. Carbonara has become very fashionable lately, with chefs at Michelin-starred restaurants making deconstructed versions of it, and food bloggers going wild over top ten lists of the best carbonara in Rome. Unfortunately it's just as easy to get a bad dish of carbonara as a good one. The key, as always, is the quality of the ingredients. The guanciale and eggs need to be the best, since they provide all the flavor.

Bucatini all'Amatriciana: Thick strands of hollow pasta dressed with a rich sauce of tomatoes and guanciale. Be careful, since bucatini can be the most dangerous of pastas to eat. The thick strands of tomato-coated pasta tend to flip back and forth uncontrollably as they work their way to your mouth, making the front of your shirt look like a Jackson Pollock painting. This is the time to tuck that napkin into your collar.

when in rome . . .
rules for eating pasta

1. *No bread:* Since pasta is a starch, bread is never eaten with this course.

2. *Don't cut!:* If you order long pasta, like spaghetti, bucatini, or fettuccine, please don't cut it. It's meant to be twirled on your fork. Practice makes perfect.

3. *Easy on the cheese:* Most trattorie serve pasta with just enough cheese already on it. Even if a little dish of cheese is served on the side, don't overdo it. Romans don't.

eating pasta in rome

It is almost impossible to find a restaurant in Rome that doesn't serve pasta. That said, here are a handful of my favorites where I go for a specific dish.

Sora Margherita
Piazza delle Cinque Scole 30,
39-06-687-4216
➤ Their unique take on cacio e pepe: handmade fettuccine, Pecorino Romano, black

pepper, and a massive dollop of fresh ricotta.

Perilli

Via Marmorata, 39-06-575-5100

➤ My favorite carbonara in Rome. I'm also partial to their rigatoni with a sauce made from *coda alla vaccinara,* or "oxtail."

Trattoria Monti

Via San Vito 15A, 39-06-446-6573

➤ Although it's not typically Roman, sometimes you want something different. I go to Trattoria Monti for their famous tortolloni, a huge type of ravioli stuffed with ricotta and a barely cooked egg yolk.

Danilo

Via A. Petrarca, 39-06-772-00111

➤ Although almost all Roman trattorie serve gnocchi on Thursdays, Danilo adds their own special twist. Rather than serving gnocchi *al ragù,* they dress them with a pesto made from pistachios and flavored with chunks of guanciale.

recipes

swiss chard gnudi

(See the photograph on page 87.)

Serves 4

I already admitted that when it comes to making pasta, I'm a disaster. I'm talking about traditional egg and flour pasta that gets rolled out superthin and cut into sheets or strips to make lasagna or fettuccine. But I am kind of crafty, and like forming things with my hands, which is why I like making gnocchi. They can definitely be lumped in the pasta category, are handmade, but are much more forgiving in terms of eventual success. And they are superimpressive, which I love.

This is a recipe for gnudi, which you can think of as either ravioli filling without the ravioli (and *gnudi* does mean "naked") or a potatoless version of gnocchi. You can play around with the ingredients (my friend Evan makes amazingly beautiful pink ones using beets), and if you don't get the proportions quite right, they are very forgiving. Although they look kind of fussy, once you get going they shape up pretty quickly.

> 2 cups cooked Swiss chard
>
> 3 garlic cloves, unpeeled
>
> 1½ cups drained, fresh whole-milk ricotta
>
> ½ cup grated Parmesan cheese
>
> 1 teaspoon salt
>
> Freshly ground black pepper
>
> 1 cup (100 grams) all-purpose flour
>
> 6 tablespoons (¾ stick/90 grams) unsalted butter
>
> 8 fresh sage leaves

This is the kind of recipe you really want to use fresh vegetables for. Although I realize that frozen spinach can be a godsend, try to up the ante here. And do

(continued)

feel free to experiment with other kinds of veggies. I mentioned beets earlier, but you can also use zucchini or leafy greens. The important thing to remember is that once you have cooked them, you want to let them drain as much as possible to get the water out. If you're using greens, grab them and really squeeze the moisture out. Ditto for the ricotta. This should be drained of as much liquid as possible.

Rinse and wilt the Swiss chard in barely enough boiling water to cover the bottom of the pan. Place the unpeeled garlic cloves on top of the greens, so that they steam as well. When the vegetables are cooked, drain them. Pick out the garlic cloves and peel them.

Place the Swiss chard, peeled garlic, and ricotta in a food processor and process until smooth.

Transfer the mixture to a bowl and add the Parmesan cheese, salt, and pepper and stir to combine well. Start adding the flour, ¼ cup at a time, mixing well. You may not need all of it; it will depend on how wet your veggies and ricotta are. The aim is to use as little flour as necessary and only enough to hold things together.

With floured hands gently form the dough into small oval-shaped gnudi. Each one should use about a tablespoon of the mix. Place on floured baking sheet.

Bring a large pot of salted water to a boil.

Melt the butter in a small pan. Add the

sage and let it sizzle for a minute. Remove from the heat.

Cook the gnudi in the pot of salted water as you would gnocchi. You'll probably have to cook them in about three batches. Gently slip them into the boiling water, then as soon as they bob to the surface, in 3 to 4 minutes, scoop them up and out with a slotted spoon. Transfer them to a heated dish while you cook the remaining gnudi.

To serve place the gnudi in individual dishes and spoon over the sage butter. Top with extra grated Parmesan cheese.

carbonara

(See the opposite page, in the background.)

Serves 4 to 5

I know I repeat this over and over, but with these simple recipes, ingredients make all the difference. If you can get imported pasta, then use it here. I love Faella, which comes from Gragnano, outside of Naples. As for guanciale, I know it's hard to find, but do try. If you have to substitute thick-cut bacon, that's OK, but not smoked, and definitely not lean! (You want that fat.) Eggs are the main ingredient here, and you will be eating them raw. So make them farmers' market fresh please, if possible.

Although I use a sharp Pecorino Romano for dishes like cacio e pepe and

(continued)

amatriciana, for my carbonara I actually prefer the milder taste of Parmigiano-Reggiano. I know it's not 100 percent traditional, but it may make things easier for you, since good Pecorino Romano is hard to find.

1 tablespoon extra-virgin olive oil
6 ounces (150 grams) guanciale, cut into small cubes
1 pound (500 grams) rigatoni
4 egg yolks
1 egg white
½ cup grated Parmigiano-Reggiano or mild Pecorino Romano cheese
Freshly ground black pepper

Heat a pan large enough to hold all the pasta over medium heat, and pour in the olive oil. Add the guanciale and cook just until it starts to render its fat and get crisp at the edges; you want it to stay chewy, and not get brown and hard like bacon. Turn off heat, and do I have to say it? Do not drain the fat? Well, I'll say it: Do not drain the fat. This is one of the main ingredients of this dish. If you want something with no pork fat, this dish isn't for you.

Put the egg yolks and egg white in a large serving bowl, Beat just enough to break up the yolks. Add the grated cheese and pepper and mix well with a fork to create a creamy "sauce." I find this is the secret to a great carbonara, mixing the grated cheese with the eggs before you add the pasta.

Bring a large pot of salted water to a boil. Add the pasta and cook until on the hard side of al dente; you will be adding the pasta to the hot guanciale and also letting it sit a bit with the egg-cheese mixture, so you don't want to overcook it.

In the meantime, reheat the guanciale.

Drain the pasta, reserving ½ cup of the hot pasta cooking water. Add the drained pasta to the pan with the guanciale, stirring and making sure you coat the pasta well with the contents of the pan.

Turn off heat and transfer the pasta to the bowl with the egg-cheese mixture. Toss well, adding a bit of the reserved pasta cooking water if you think it is too thick. Cover the bowl with a lid, and let sit for 2 minutes to let the eggs set a bit. Remove the lid, stir one more time, and serve.

cacio e pepe with arugula

Serves 4 to 5

I can't help futzing with classics. Which is why, nine times out of ten, I add some sort of green to the classic cacio e pepe. Here is the recipe, which you are welcome to futz with as you see fit, adding any other kind of green at the last minute.

Ideally you should use a hard-grating pecorino. In a pinch, you can use Parmesan, but it will have a different taste—sweeter and less strong. The trick is to find a cheese that is hard and with a high fat content so that it melts without clumping.

- 1 pound (500 grams) pasta (I like rigatoni)
- 1½ cups grated Pecorino Romano cheese
- 2 tablespoons freshly ground black pepper, or more to taste
- 2 bunches arugula, washed and roughly chopped

Bring a large pot of salted water to a boil. Add the pasta and cook until al dente.

Drain the pasta, reserving 1 cup of the pasta cooking water. Transfer the pasta to a large, heated bowl. Sprinkle on ½ cup of the cheese and toss, adding ¼ cup of the reserved pasta water. Mix well, adding the pepper and the rest of the cheese and as much water as you need to keep it all moist. You don't want it watery, but you do want it creamy. Quickly mix in the greens, distributing them well.

Serve immediately. This pasta starts to seize up right away, so you want everyone seated at the table as you drain the pasta. Some restaurants in Rome, like Danilo and Felice, even make a big show of preparing the dish in front of the table.

{ chapter 10 }

stocking my pantry

f you read my blog, you might have the impression that I am superorganized, always have three meals on the table, and manage to photograph and write about every one. You'd be very wrong.

Actually, I used to be very organized. From the time I was in high school, when I was in charge of cooking for our family, I would research out all the menus, make a grocery list, and have everything planned and ready for the week. This continued in university, where I cooked not only for myself but also for my roommates. While I let them decide what they would take with them for lunch each day, dinners were my domain and *The Moosewood Cookbook* was my bible. Graduate school was easier, since I was on my own and had no one to boss around. I was the master planner, and mealtimes ran like clockwork.

And even during my first few years of marriage and small children, I was a fan of weeklong meal plans accompanied by detailed shopping lists. I was always prepared.

I'm not so sure when this all started to fall apart. But at some point, my lazy nature began to assert itself. Actually, it wasn't that I was lazy, just that I was busy doing other things (like writing books) and so my mealtime organizational skills fell by the wayside. Thank god my passion for shopping saved me from complete disaster.

When it comes to Italian pantry items, I am a shopaholic. I admit it. If it has a cute label, then there is a good chance I will buy it. So my pantry is always pretty much stocked to overflowing. While I may think I have nothing in the house to prepare for dinner, I'm always wrong. I can invariably wrangle something from the cans, bags, and boxes that fill up my cupboard.

I love the word for pantry in Italian: *dispensa*. Usually in Italian, words have very specific meaning, but *dispensa* has three, all of which I believe apply to me, and particularly at that time of day when dinnertime is looming. The first definition of *dispensa* is "pantry." I've been attached to the word *pantry* ever since I fell in love with *Little House on the Prairie*. There was never a meal laid on the rough wooden table that didn't involve a trip to Ma's pantry. I dreamed that one day I, too, would have my own little house (not necessarily on the prairie) with a well-stocked pantry from which comforting, nourishing meals would somehow miraculously begin.

The second meaning of *dispensa* is one I learned only recently, when sitting in on Italian cooking school classes. At the beginning of the class the teacher would pass out a sheet of paper that was called the *dispensa*. Listing not only the ingredients and recipes, the paper would also outline exactly what we'd be learning over the course of the class. While no one is handing me a list of instructions when I go to make dinner, I like to think that my well-stocked

pantry is somehow advising me, letting me know what we will be covering for tonight's dinner.

And finally, *dispensa* also translates as "dispensation," as in "you are forgiven" (in the Catholic religion or in a legal kind of way), or not having to adhere to any previously agreed upon rules, which is kind of a nice idea when dinner comes around.

One of the reasons that my pantry is so well stocked is my constant fear of never being able to find that special ingredient ever again. I am a complete and utter sucker for the handmade, artisanal, heritage, and limited-production food product. If there is a farmers' market, I am there. And there isn't an Italian food fair that I haven't been to many times over. When I'm walking around the aisles of Slow Food's Salone del Gusto in Torino, or the Taste fair in Florence, I'm there to do research, to discover the latest and most obscure. I taste my way through things like pickled garlic shoots, Sardinian smoked fish roe, and cheeses aged in mountaintop caves. While many of the things I try are there only for the tasting, even more are for sale, and I'm sure that one of the reasons I have shoulder problems is due to my tendency to overload my shopping bags with kilos of beans, cans of fish, and bottles of balsamic that get lugged on the train, back to Rome, to fill my dispensa.

So even though I am past the days when I would make up detailed meal plans for the week, I don't really have to worry, since without really even trying, my cupboard is rarely bare.

best places to stock up your pantry in rome

Castroni

Via Nazionale 71, 39-06-489-8744

➤ Castroni is where you go in Rome when you can't find that hard-to-get essential ingredient. Cranberries for Thanksgiving? Check. Soba noodles? Check. The sprawling store off Cola di Rienzo (and the newly located store on Via Nazionale) is where expats—and Romans—go for exotic and foreign goodies. But it also has one of the best selections of Italian pantry items like olive oil, balsamic vinegar, mostarda, coffee, and chocolates.

Eataly

Piazzale XII, Ottobre 1492, 39-06-902-79201

➤ One-stop shopping for just about everything an Italian pantry could want, from olive oil–packed tuna to artisanal pasta.

D.O.L.

Via Domenico Panaroli 6, 39-06-2430-0765

➤ This small shop, located outside of Rome's center in the Tuscolana neighborhood, is run by the passionate Vincenzo Macino, who has made it his personal goal to revive and make available, commercially and sustainably, the food of Lazio. In addition to cheese and cured meats, you'll find plenty to fill your pantry: olive oils, vinegars, dried pastas, jams, and legumes.

Emporio delle Spezie

Via Luca della Robbia 20, 39-327-861-2655

➤ One of the best spice stores in Rome is located in the Testaccio neighborhood.

stocking your italian pantry

Extra-Virgin Olive Oil. This is your basic ingredient, so make it count. Don't assume that the olive oil you buy in the supermarket that is labeled extra-virgin Italian olive oil is that. If it's cheap, then chances are that it's either not extra virgin or not even Italian. The best way to get the best olive oil is to go to a trusted source.

Anchovies. The best come in clear glass jars, to better display the fat fillets. You can use those packed either in salt or in oil. I use and love both, for different reasons. If I have more time, then I'll make the effort to use those in salt. They are fiddly since they involve soaking, and then filleting, but the large sturdy fillets are beautiful. On the other hand, if you find good-quality fillets packed in olive oil, that is so much easier. The only problem is that they usually cost a bit more.

Capers. The best capers come from the islands around Sicily, Pantelleria, and the Aeolian Islands. If you can find them packed in salt, get those, since they have a much purer taste than those packed in brine or vinegar. They just need a soak (or a parboil) to remove the excess salt.

Tuna. I consider water-packed tuna to be the equivalent of boneless, skinless chicken breasts. In other words, why bother? High-quality olive oil–packed tuna is a thing of beauty and delicious, and an essential component of any well-stocked pantry. Ventresca, or belly tuna, is the best. Known as *toro* in sushi restaurants, the canned version is supertender, flavorful, and rich. It's also pricey, so you might just want to use regular oil-packed tuna.

Beans. Dried beans are always going to be better than canned beans, but I realize that you might have last-minute emergencies. So it's best to always have both in your pantry.

Tomatoes. If possible, try to get your hands on imported tomatoes from Italy. I always keep a variety in my pantry, including peeled (*pelati*) San Marzano, both crushed and pureed. The best, though, are canned cherry tomatoes from Sicily or around Naples.

Sardines. Tuna is not the only canned fish. You'd be amazed what a can of good sardines can add to a pasta dish.

Olives. A few jars, with pits please, of both black and green. Don't feel committed to Italian imports, since those from Turkey, Greece, Spain, and France are just as good.

Pasta. If there is one item you stock your pantry with, it should be several bags of good-quality pasta. And when I say good quality, I really do mean that. Try to buy imported pasta, which has been air-dried slowly. Industrially made pasta—especially that made in the United States—can't compare in taste or texture. Brands I like, that are available abroad: Martelli, Rustichelli, Faella, Benedetto Cavallieri, and Garafolo.

pantry rice salad

In Italy it's still pretty common to eat seasonally. No one would ever dream of having *pomodori al riso* (rice-stuffed tomatoes) or *friselle* (tomato-topped rusks) in the dead of winter because where on earth would those tomatoes come from? And anything with *cavolo nero* (kale) is for the cold months only. The eating seasonally thing is mostly tied to ingredients, obviously. But there are certain dishes that could, in theory, be made year-round but are reserved for specific seasons because, well, they just are.

Insalata di riso (rice salad) is one of those dishes. It's simply boiled rice with chopped raw vegetables as well as a few preserved ones. Add olive oil, salt, and pepper, and you've got your dish. In theory you could eat it year-round, varying it season by season with the addition of different vegetables.

But no. I think there is probably an Italian law that says insalata di riso can only be eaten during the summer. And just in case you are confused as to the official start of insalata di riso season, just take a stroll down any aisle in a supermarket and you are sure to be faced with a large display of Condiriso.

Yes. There is a specific mix of preserved vegetables that is used for insalata di riso that is available only during the summer. While I'm usually on the "fresh is better" team, like any good Italian housewife, I, too, make sure I stock up on these little jars.

But of course I've developed my own version of rice salad over the years, which manages to mix both fresh and preserved vegetables. Why include anything in a jar, you may wonder? Because I like rice salad that includes that pickle-y, briny taste. Little chunks of olives, carrots, and onions that have had a good long vinegar soak. And I always choose the *leggero,* or "light," version of Condiriso, which means the goodies are preserved in brine, not in olive oil, which makes them not only lighter, but even more sour.

I also break from traditional Italian insalata di riso tradition by using the wrong kind of rice. Most Italians use parboiled rice, which is labeled clearly *"per insalata di riso."* The grains cook up all nice and separate, with no gummy starch thing happening. But I prefer the chewiness of

arborio or *carnaroli,* which makes my insalata di riso much less *caffetteria*-style. (At least I think so.)

When do I make insalata di riso? In the summer, naturally. (I'm not that iconoclastic.) Specifically, it's become a tradition to make it on the days my sisters are arriving for their annual visits from the States. Since I never quite know exactly what time they will get to the house in Umbria from the airport in Rome, it's easier if I have something already made and waiting.

recipes

insalata di riso
{ rice salad }

Serves 8

> 3 cups (¾ liter) chicken broth
>
> 1 tablespoon salt
>
> 1 pound (½ kilo) arborio rice
>
> 1 jar Condiriso, drained
>
> 1 red bell pepper, seeded and chopped
>
> 2 carrots, peeled and chopped
>
> 2 tomatoes, chopped
>
> 2 celery stalks, chopped
>
> ¼ cup extra-virgin olive oil
>
> Juice of 1 lemon
>
> 1 cup chopped fresh flat-leaf parsley
>
> Freshly ground black pepper

Bring the chicken broth and enough water to fill a pot large enough to cook

(continued)

all the rice to a boil. Add the salt. Add the rice and cook until done but not mushy. Drain.

While the rice is cooking, put the Condoriso and chopped vegetables in a large bowl. Add the olive oil, lemon juice, and parsley.

Add the warm drained rice to the vegetable mixture. Stir and let come to room temperature. Taste and adjust the seasonings. Add as much lemon juice and freshly ground pepper as you'd like.

Note: I've actually seen Condiriso for sale in the States. Another option is to buy a jar of giardiniera, a mix of pickled vegetables like cauliflower, carrots, and celery. Just make sure you chop the larger pieces finely.

Variations: You can add just about anything else you'd like. Other herbs like basil and chives are great. Also add any other chopped raw veggies like zucchini or scallions. If you want to throw in some tuna to make it more of a one-dish meal, that works, too. Or, if you're feeling porky, thinly sliced hot dogs are often my secret ingredient. For real. Feta is lovely. And, of course, if you're feeling healthy, any sort of grain will do: brown rice, farro, even barley.

pasta with sardines and roasted tomatoes

Serves 5 to 6 as a first course

My pantry is always well stocked with fish. Not your usual cans of dry white tuna in water, but cans of delicious, oily sardines, mackerel, and fatty ventresca tuna. While the ventresca tuna can be expensive, I'm always surprised at how cheap both the sardines and the mackerel are, and equally shocked at these ingredients aren't more widely used in pasta sauces.

Last summer when my mother-in-law came to visit up in Umbria, she carefully packed in her suitcase a kilo of handmade orecchiette. Since it was summer, I had plenty of tomatoes on hand, and so roasted them at high heat to toss with the pasta. While I'd usually add a few handfuls of grated ricotta salata cheese to finish, this time I decided to skip the dairy (both Sophie and Emma are getting to be slightly lactose intolerant) in favor of one of my beautifully labeled cans of sardines.

My mother-in-law was a bit skeptical as I was dumping cans of fish onto her carefully carried, handmade, fresh orecchiette. *"Cosi'? Senza fare niente?"* ("Like that? Without doing anything to them?") Putting canned food onto pasta was obviously something only an American daughter-in-law could think up.

(continued)

All doubts faded away once she tasted the pasta. *Non e' male.* ("Not bad.") From an Italian mother-in-law? That's more or less the equivalent of two Michelin stars.

2 pounds (1 kilo) fresh plum or cherry tomatoes

Salt

Hot red pepper flakes

3 teaspoons dried oregano

6 garlic cloves, thinly sliced

⅓ cup (70 milliliters) extra-virgin olive oil

1 pound (500 grams) pasta (I used orecchiette, but you can use any other pasta)

3.8-ounce (110-gram) can good-quality sardines

A handful of fresh basil leaves

Preheat the oven to 400°F (200°C).

Slice the tomatoes in half lengthwise. Lay them on a baking sheet in one layer, cut side facing up. (You may need two baking sheets.)

Sprinkle with salt, red pepper flakes, and oregano. Slip the sliced garlic into the tomatoes and drizzle liberally with olive oil; the more the better. Roast in the oven until the tomatoes have begun to shrivel up and brown, about 45 minutes.

In the meantime, bring a large pot of salted water to a boil. When the tomatoes are almost done, boil the pasta, cooking until al dente. Drain, reserving ½ cup of the pasta cooking water. Transfer the pasta to a large bowl, and scrape the tomatoes onto the pasta. Pour the reserved hot pasta water onto the baking sheet(s), and use it to scrape up the bits of browned tomatoes and their juices. Pour that on the pasta as well and toss to combine. Add the sardines to the pasta, breaking them up with a wooden spoon. Add the fresh basil and serve.

cavatelli with tuna and lemon

Serves 5

Most people take tuna for granted. It's that can you keep in the pantry for an emergency. And if you're like most, you sort of think of tuna as a relatively inexpensive diet food, and so buy the small cans packed in water, which taste about as interesting as cat food.

But there's a whole other world of tuna out there. Ventresca tuna is from the belly, and so is very tender, very fatty, and extremely flavorful. It's always packaged in flat cans to preserve the shape of the fillets, and always packed in olive oil. And, for some reason, the old-fashioned cans always have fantastically beautiful labels, which makes me overbuy.

Although you don't have to add much to a can of fine tuna to turn it into a topping for pasta, you probably also have lemons, capers, and olives around, which make it even better.

1 pound (500 grams) cavatelli

Salt

16 black olives, pitted

2 tablespoons capers

2 garlic cloves, crushed

¼ cup extra-virgin olive oil

½ teaspoon hot red pepper flakes

Grated zest and juice of 1 untreated
    lemon

One 3.5-ounce (100-gram) can imported
    ventresca tuna

½ cup chopped fresh flat-leaf parsley

Bring a large pot of salted water to boil, add the pasta, and cook until al dente.

Meanwhile, in a large bowl combine the olives, capers, garlic, oil, red pepper flakes, lemon zest, and juice and stir well. Add the tuna, broken into large chunks.

When the pasta is al dente, drain, reserving ½ cup of the pasta cooking water. Transfer the pasta to the bowl with the tuna mixture and toss gently. Add a bit of the reserved cooking water to moisten. Add the chopped parsley, toss, and serve.

strong tomato sauce

Serves 5

One of the biggest property owners in my pantry is the jars and jars of tomatoes that our friend Paolo puts up every August and gives to us. People so often think about these "canned things" as somehow not vegetables anymore, but just a vehicle for sauce. And the other misconception that people have is that pasta is not a diet food. The evil carbohydrate raises its head.

But diet is about how much you eat, of course. If you eat loads of pasta (or anything, for that matter), you're going to gain weight. And if you load tons of oil and cheese on top of that, well . . . you know where this is going.

So, here follows my answer to what to make when your pantry is bare and you maybe want to start the year on a slightly lighter note. Things to note: I've cut the oil way down, which isn't always the way I do things. But in this case I've doubled the amount of tomatoes I usually use and cooked them down even more to boost flavor. And to add more zing, I've thrown in a handful of olives—not too many, just a few to give texture and color and a bit of "oliveyness." I've also added anchovies, so yes, this is really *puttanesca* (but with less oil, which I consider one of the main ingredients of puttanesca sauce).

And a word about amounts of pasta. It bears repeating about the whole quantity thing. More pasta equals more calories. Now, I don't know about your family, but in mine as much pasta as gets cooked gets eaten. So like a good Italian cook I measure out my pasta. For a dish like this, with such a light sauce, I use

(continued)

100 grams (3½ ounces) per person. (No more than that.) For a heavier sauce, or one with a lot more vegetables, I cut it back to 75 (2.6 ounces) or even 50 grams (1.7 ounces) a person.

- 4 teaspoons extra-virgin olive oil
- 6 garlic cloves, chopped
- ½ teaspoon hot red pepper flakes
- 4 anchovies
- 8 black olives, pitted
- 4 cups pelati (peeled whole San Marzano tomatoes) with their juices
- 2 cups canned crushed tomatoes
- 1 pound (500 grams) farfalle (see note)
- About ½ cup chopped fresh flat-leaf parsley

Heat the olive oil over medium heat in a pan large enough to hold all the cooked pasta and sauce. Add the garlic and cook for just a couple of minutes, then add the red pepper flakes, anchovies, and olives. Cook, stirring, until the anchovies start to fall apart, about 2 minutes.

Add the tomatoes and their juices. This will seem like a lot of tomatoes and juices, but you're really going to cook it down a lot. Turn the heat to medium-high and let the sauce really bubble away. You may have to put one of those splatter shields on the pot, but you don't want to cover it. You want the sauce to reduce to about one-fourth of what you started with. This should take only about 20 minutes or so, if you are really cooking on medium-high heat.

In the meantime, bring a large pot of salted water to a boil and cook the pasta until al dente. Drain, add the pasta to the sauce in the pan, and cook until heated through, scraping in any bits of dried sauce that have stuck to the sides of the pan.

Top with parsley and serve.

Note: Of course you can use another shape of pasta. But sometimes I feel as if I'm getting into a penne rut.

bean and tuna salad

Serves 4

During the summer, I like to make up a big bowl of some type of salad on Sunday, to have something to see us through a week of lunches. More often than not it's a grain or rice salad. And of course, the perennial standby: bean and tuna salad.

While I usually add something bright and colorful like bell peppers or cherry tomatoes to a bean salad, I am often forced to raid the pantry. An excellent can of olive oil–packed tuna and a beautiful red onion from Tropea come to the rescue. A hefty pour of olive oil and some freshly ground black pepper turn it all into a light, yet delicious, Sunday lunch, with plenty left over to see us through at least three more lunches during the week.

2 cups dried beans (see note)
One 8.8-ounce (250-gram) can olive oil–
    packed tuna
1 large red onion, chopped
1 big bunch flat-leaf parsley, leaves
    roughly chopped
Salt
Freshly ground black pepper
Extra-virgin olive oil

Put the drained cooked beans into a large bowl. Open the tuna and add it to the beans, along with the olive oil it is packed in. (Come on, you can do it. Don't drain that good, tuna-flavored oil away!)

Add the onion and parsley, and stir. Season with salt and abundant black pepper to taste. You may need a bit more olive oil.

This is the basic version. If you do end up making it to have for lunches during the week, then each day you can add something else to change things up. A sliced tomato is always great. Some chopped bell peppers. I also love celery. It's up to you.

Note: Beans: Yes, you can use canned beans. But as always, dried are so much better (or fresh if you can get them). If you are using dried beans, soak them for at least 6 hours, then cook in abundant salted water just until tender. Do not overcook. When you're making bean salad, a bit of a bite is a good thing, and you definitely want to avoid the mush factor.

bringing home the pancetta

S ome husbands come home to their wives with a bunch of tulips or a box of chocolates. My husband? He's more likely to lug home a wheel of pecorino, a bag of dried peppers, or a crate full of lemons. Because he figured out early on that if he brought me something to cook with, it was a win-win for everyone. I'd be thrilled to have some incredibly delicious ingredient to play with. And Domenico? Well, he's the very happy beneficiary of all that playing around.

While it didn't take Domenico long to figure out I preferred sausages and dried cannellini beans to earrings and perfume, he's definitely refined his gift giving over the years. While his travels certainly dictate what he comes back home with (chocolate from Switzerland, lemons from Amalfi, and pistachios from Sicily), there is one ingredient that has hogged its way to the front lines: pork. Nine times out of ten, my husband comes home with some kind of pig. He takes the phrase "bringing home the bacon" very seriously.

I have a few theories about why Domenico comes home with pork as a gift more often than anything else. First of all there is the fact that most of Domenico's architectural restoration projects take place in central Italy, in Umbria and Tuscany. This is big pork-eating country, and many of the contractors or farmers Domenico comes into contact with not only raise their own animals but also take great pride in curing pancetta, guanciale, and prosciutto.

Domenico also loves shopping. So when he's out at a work site in Tuscany or Umbria, he'll always discover the most famous butcher in the area, and go on a shopping spree. And since he can't leave freshly butchered pork chops in a car that will sit around all day, cured meat will do just fine. And here he doesn't limit himself to the expected pancetta or guanciale. The stranger, the better is Domenico's motto when it comes to shopping at the butcher's.

While I don't accompany Domenico on these shopping forays, it's as if I'm there, since he phones me at least a dozen times to make sure he's getting the right things. My input is usually about quantity. "No, we really only need one prosciutto. Really. One will be more than enough."

But somehow this never happens. Domenico often gets into a pork-buying frenzy and the result is that my refrigerator is almost always full of huge slabs of cured pork. Even though I end up giving bits and pieces to my friends, I'm still left with a lot of lard to work through.

I know right now you're probably getting a bit worried about the state of our arteries. But along the way I've adopted the Italian method of using pork as a seasoning. Yes. Everything tastes better with a bit of pork added to it.

We are not huge consumers of meat in our household. Vegetables, pastas, grains, and beans make up a large percentage of our dinners. But I figured out early on what most Italians already know: A little bit of pork fat can go a long way in making an ordinary plate of almost anything extraordinary. And I'm not talking about having bacon for breakfast every morning.

This philosophy is actually tied not to an abundance of pork (or any kind of meat, for that matter) but rather to a lack of it. *Cucina povera*, "poor cooking," was a way to take inexpensive ingredients and not only make them taste better, but add much-needed calories to a dish that was otherwise pretty meager. In this way one small chunk of pancetta could be added to a vegetable dish, making it not only more savory, but more filling as well.

cured pork and travel

Until May 2013, it was strictly forbidden to import any type of pork into the United States from Italy. The law dated to the times when trichinosis and other pork-borne pathogens were a real issue. These days there is no more danger of developing lockjaw from a slice of prosciutto, so the USDA has finally begun to open the borders. As of the writing of this book, you still must have an official import permit, so sticking that salami in your suitcase is still off-limits. But keep your eyes out for further loosening of the law, as well as a slew of Italian imports.

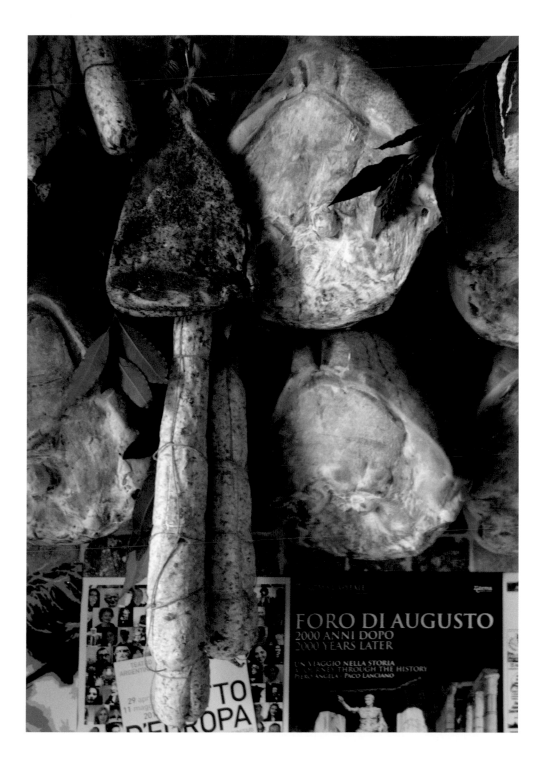

guanciale versus pancetta

One of the best investments that you can make, in terms of stocking up your pork larder, is a big chunk of pancetta or guanciale. Both are cuts of cured pork, and are often compared to and translated as bacon.

Pancetta: Cured pork belly.

Guanciale: Cured pork jowl.

Guanciale, which in Italy has a greater ratio of lean to fat, has a stronger pork flavor than pancetta and is the cut that is traditionally used in Roman pasta dishes like carbonara, gricia, and amatriciana. But don't get overly upset if you can't find it; pancetta will do just fine. If you must substitute bacon, use one that is not smoked, and if you can find slab bacon all the better, since you want to cut it in chunks, not flimsy strips.

Storing: My neighbors in Umbria store their cured pork in a cold cellar, hanging it from the ceiling. I'm sure it keeps just fine, but since our home in Rome is too warm, I stash mine in the refrigerator. A well-cured piece of pancetta or guanciale will keep for a few months, if you treat it well. Wrap it in a piece of paper towel and then cover it with a piece of loosely wrapped aluminum foil. Do not wrap it in any type of plastic, since that will encourage mold. Don't worry if the pork gets a bit dried out; it will still taste good.

when in rome . . . eating pork

- Don't miss the following pasta dishes, which feature guanciale: pasta alla gricia, spaghetti alla carbonara, and bucatini all'amatriciana

- Stop by Norcineria Viola (Campo de' Fiori) for a full-on pork immersion.

- Many *alimentari* (delicatessens) will prepare simple sandwiches on the spot for you. Just choose your meat, and they'll split open a fresh roll, and fill it up with salami, prosciutto, or mortadella.

recipes

I've become a master of making something out of almost nothing. And I never throw leftovers away. Even if there is one lonely slice of mortadella left, I will carefully wrap it up because I know it will come in handy. The following recipes call for minimal amounts of cured pork. But let me make myself very clear: Although the amount may be small, the impact is big. So, to answer your question: You can't make these recipes without the cured pork. Well, you can, but then you might as well just skip over this chapter.

green beans with mortadella salad

Serves 4–5

I'm not quite sure how I ended up buying a pound of green beans in the middle of winter, but they were thoroughly uninspiring; so uninspiring that they sat in the refrigerator for a good long week, getting less and less interesting, before I could think of cooking them. By the end of the week, there they were, the lone vegetable left in the fridge, waiting to be cooked for Saturday lunch, before the weekly trip to the market.

Luckily, mortadella came to the rescue. An itty-bitty piece of mortadella, left over from a cured meat tasting I led, was the inspiration for this pork-infused, green bean salad. And I have to say, that little bit of pork did a lot to the I-don't-want-to-know-where-they-come-from winter green beans. It added just the right touch of pig to an otherwise very veggie dish.

The trick to this dish is to prepare all the ingredients in the serving bowl while the beans are cooking. You want to add the beans to the dressing while they are still piping hot, so that they sort of cook the shallots and garlic, and coax the fat nodules out of the mortadella.

I actually make a similar version of this dish all summer long, using a mixture of tomatoes and basil with garlic and red onions. The same goes for this: Place piping hot green beans into dressing.

1 pound (½ kilo) green beans, cleaned
1 slice mortadella (about ½ cup chopped in small pieces)
1 shallot, finely chopped
1 garlic clove, crushed
2 tablespoons extra-virgin olive oil
2 tablespoons chopped fresh tarragon
Zest of 1 lemon, peeled with a potato peeler and finely chopped
Zest of 1 small orange, peeled with a potato peeler and finely chopped
3 tablespoons fresh lemon juice
2 tablespoons fresh orange juice
Salt
Freshly ground black pepper
¼ cup chopped, roasted almonds

Steam the green beans until tender.

Meanwhile, place the mortadella, shallot, garlic, olive oil, tarragon, chopped citrus zests, and citrus juices in a large bowl and stir to mix well.

When the beans are tender, drain them and then add them, still steaming hot, to the mixture in the bowl. Toss well and season with salt and pepper to taste.

Let cool, toss again, and top with the almonds. Serve at room temperature.

roasted radicchio and cured pork

Serves 4–5

You know how everyone is always writing recipes that use up leftover bits of cheese? What I want to know is why doesn't anyone ever address the even more pressing issue of half-forgotten, unloved, leftover bits of dried-out salami and random bits of cured meats.

Am I the only one with this problem? You know. Nubs of boar sausage; slightly dried chunks of pancetta; a piece of duck prosciutto you were saving for a special occasion that never came.

I decided to use these odds and ends and adapt them to a recipe that my friend Judy makes called radicchio roses. Actually, I adapted the recipe instead of following it faithfully, mostly because I had forgotten to buy one of the key ingredients. While I'd picked up a couple of gorgeous heads of radicchio at the farmers' market on Saturday, somehow I forgot to buy some sausage, which left me with no porky stuffing . . . until I remembered those nubs.

They all went into my mini chopper, which has an incredibly strong motor. Within a minute my various fatty bits were looking pretty similar to the sausage Judy's recipe had originally called for.

While I was filling my basket at the market, I couldn't quite remember which kind of radicchio Judy's recipe called for.

So I got a head of very loose *radicchio di Treviso*, as well as the tighter *radicchio di Chioggia*. They both worked perfectly.

Radicchio, when cooked, is a marvelous thing. All bitterness disappears, and the edges of the leaves get brown and crispy and extra sweet, which is the perfect foil for all that pork.

I think using the raw sausage called for in the original recipe probably results in a softer consistency. But me? There's nothing I like better than crunchy bits of browned and crisped cured meats.

Take that, leftover pork nubs.

¼ pound (130 grams) leftover cured pork, roughly chopped (see note)
2 heads radicchio
Extra-virgin olive oil, for drizzling
Salt
Freshly ground black pepper

Preheat the oven to 350°F (180°C). Lightly oil a baking sheet.

Place all the roughly chopped cured meat in a food processor and pulse until it looks like ground meat.

WARNING: At this point you may be tempted to just eat all that lovely pink, salty, fatty salami mush schmeared on a piece of bread. Resist.

If you are using the loose-leaf kind of radicchio, then just rinse and dry well, keeping the head intact. Then stuff bits of the sausage in between the leaves. If you are using the tighter Chioggia radicchio, cut it into quarters, through the stem end, keeping that part intact. Lay the pieces on the tray and gently stuff bits of the sausage between the leaves.

About the stuffing: Just stick the stuff in, here and there. Think of the pork as more of a condiment than a main course. Drizzle liberally with olive oil, and season with salt and pepper.

Bake for about 30 minutes. The radicchio should be fully cooked, and the edges of the radicchio leaves well browned.

Note: Of course you can make this with anything. I used a mix of boar sausage, pancetta, Calabrian spicy salami, and a small bit of fennel sausage from Tuscany (I think that's where it came from . . .).

cauliflower and blood sausage

Serves 4–5

One day Domenico, while up in Tuscany visiting a construction site, called me on the phone, all excited. "I got a *buristo*!"

First of all, you have to realize that Domenico loves calling me from the speaker phone in the car. The problem is, he's usually driving in the back hills of Umbria or Tuscany, which means bad reception . . . which means I usually get about half of what he's said.

After he had repeated *buristo* about

five times, I finally just said, "Great! fantastic!," hung up the phone, and decided to Google what I thought I had heard.

Buristo: A pig's stomach stuffed with pig's blood and pork.

I must have misheard. I couldn't imagine Domenico was going to arrive home with a blood-stuffed pig's stomach. Actually, he arrived with just half a blood-stuffed pig's stomach.

I have to admit that I had never bought blood sausage before. Tasted it, for sure, many, many times, at food fairs and salami stores. And I did always like it. It's so rich, and usually so strong tasting, that by the time I'd tasted it I'd usually decided that I'd had enough. After searching around the Web a bit, I saw that buristo, a Tuscan specialty, is often used on top of bruschetta, which sounded like a great idea. The over-the-top richness would melt into the hot and toasted bread.

Since I had two beautiful heads of cauliflower to use, I decided to make a kind of carbless bruschetta. I took the cauliflower and cut it into thick, steaklike, slabs. After brushing them with olive oil and a bit of salt and pepper, I laid a slice of buristo on top of each one. Into a hot oven they went, and 20 minutes later the cauliflower had softened and browned at the edges and the buristo had melted into all the nooks and crevices.

(continued)

The great thing about using pork as a condiment? It almost makes you forget you aren't eating any carbs.

1 head cauliflower

Extra-virgin olive oil, for drizzling

Salt

Freshly ground black pepper

Several slices buristo (see note)

A handful of chopped fresh flat-leaf
parsley

Preheat the oven to 400°F (200°C). Line a baking sheet with parchment paper.

Cut the cauliflower into ⅗-inch-thick slices, being careful to keep the "steaks" together. This is easy in the center, where the stem holds everything together. If you are serving this for company, it might be worth it to get several heads of cauliflower and use only the center parts. Then reserve the side pieces for another use.

Place the cauliflower steaks on the prepared baking sheet. Drizzle liberally with olive oil, coating both sides. Sprinkle with salt and pepper. Lay a thin slice of sausage on top of each steak, covering it. (You may have to use more than one slice if your cauliflower is big.)

Bake in the oven, on the middle rack, until tender and slightly browned, about 20 minutes.

Serve sprinkled with chopped parsley.

Note: I'd never seen buristo before, so I'm thinking it might be hard for you to track down. You can substitute any other type of blood sausage, like Spanish morcilla, French boudin noir, or even German blutwurst.

bruschetta with wild asparagus and pancetta

Makes 6 bruschetti

Having a slab of pancetta to work your way through forces you to think about old favorite recipes in new ways. The easiest—and maybe the best—recipe I came up with was this simple bruschetta. I'm not sure why, but up until now I'd never considered using pancetta for bruschetta. I guess mostly because I never had an entire slab of pancetta to play around with before.

While I used wild asparagus (which was fabulous), you can certainly use regular asparagus, or any other veggie, for that matter. The key, in any variation, is crunchy, chewy bits of pancetta along with the pork fat soaking into the bread.

½ cup cubed pancetta

1 bunch wild asparagus, tender parts only (see note)

Salt

Freshly ground black pepper

6 slices crusty Italian bread, sliced about ½ inch thick

1 garlic clove, peeled

Extra-virgin olive oil, for drizzling

Heat a medium frying pan over medium heat, and add the pancetta. Cook, until it's rendered its fat and become crisp.

Remove from the fat with a slotted spoon and transfer to a small bowl. (Do not put it on a paper towel. You want to retain all that good pork fat!)

Add the cut-up asparagus to the pan with the rendered pancetta fat and stir. Sprinkle with salt (how much will depend on how salty your pancetta is) and pepper. Cook, adding a bit of water if necessary, until tender. Add the pancetta, with its juices, back into the pan and stir to combine.

Toast the bread, over an open fire if possible. If not, then over the flames of your stovetop, or in a toaster.

While the bread is still hot, rub it with garlic and drizzle with a bit of olive oil. Divide the asparagus mixture evenly among the slices of bread and serve.

Note: Asparagus come in all shapes and sizes. Wild asparagus have the least amount of tender, edible stalk to them, only about the upper 4 inches, near the tip. Cultivated asparagus are tenderer farther down. To determine how much to use, just start chopping the asparagus into 1-inch pieces. As soon as it becomes difficult to chop or slice easily, that is the point of too tough. And remember, you can substitute about 3 cups of any other kind of vegetable like zucchini, regular asparagus, peas, fava beans, or even tender green beans, for the wild asparagus.

eating the whole animal

was never one of those kids who didn't eat liver. In fact, the main reason that I loved Jewish holidays was not the chance to run wild with my cousins, but the opportunity to gorge myself on my grandmother's chopped chicken liver. Served in a massive cut-crystal bowl that came out only for the high holidays, the creamy mixture of liver with eggs and onions sautéed in schmaltz was something I looked forward to all year long.

It was not until I moved to Florence that my love affair with offal truly blossomed. I had seen the stands all over the city selling sandwiches, but hadn't really given them much thought.

But one day, while taking a late morning *passeggiata*, Domenico suggested we detour to Piazza del Cimatori for a *panino di lampredotto*. Since I had just met Domenico, and was head over heels in love, if he had said, "Let's jump into the Arno," I probably would have done that, too. So tripe on a bun seemed a reasonable request.

The stand was crowded, and we waited our turn. When we got to the front, the tripe man asked, *"Poppo o lampredotto?"* ("Udder or stomach?") After Domenico made some sort of crude cow boob joke, we went classic, chose *lampredotto,* and the vendor stuck his long metal fork into a steaming vat of broth, pulled out a beige piece of slightly gelatinous meat, and plopped it on the cutting board.

Working quickly with a knife, he chopped up two portions' worth into thin strips, laid them atop a pair of crusty buns, sprinkled them generously with salt and pepper, and then capped them with the bun top, which had first been dunked briefly in a bit of the tripe broth.

And that was when I realized: Not only did I love Domenico, but I also really loved tripe. And maybe I loved Domenico that much more for introducing me to what is now one of my all-time favorite snacks.

Yet it wasn't until I moved to Rome, the following year, that my real offal education and appreciation began. While I knew I loved liver, and tripe was now a friend, I was able to boldly move into other, more exotic parts of the butcher shop. I soon found that in Rome not only were there entire butchers that specialized in these cuts, there was an entire neighborhood.

Testaccio is a working-class neighborhood in Rome located just out of the historic center, along the banks of the Tiber River. In ancient Roman times this was the city's port, and a large man-made mountain constructed of discarded terra cotta storage urns bears testament to the busy trade in oil and wine. Today this grass-covered knoll towers over the now-abandoned Mattatoio.

The Mattatoio, built in 1873, was, at the time, the most modern and sophisticated slaughterhouse in Europe. The sprawling plant contained areas for herding, slaughtering, butchering, and shipping out animals like cattle, sheep, and horses. The working-class neighborhood that sprang up around it housed the workers who toiled to provide meat for the city.

It was a pretty squalid life, and one that didn't pay especially well. In fact, the workers, who probably couldn't even afford to buy the meat they were helping to process, were paid in kind. But not with the prime cuts that went out to market; instead they came home with paper-wrapped parcels of the *quinto quarto*.

The "fifth quarter" was the part of the animal that for commercial purposes didn't exist. There is no fifth quarter, since these were the cuts that were normally discarded. Intestines, spleen, liver, nerves, brains . . . it was these cuts that became an essential part of Roman cooking, and that today, once again, are showing up on menus all over the city.

If, as a child, I came to equate Jewish high holidays with chopped chicken liver, in my new life in Rome (and with my non-Jewish husband) we celebrate pretty much every holiday that comes along and it seems I still have a tendency to lean toward the offal side of things.

I know people like Easter in Italy for a lot of reasons: Some like the big chocolate eggs, others the cheese-filled *pizza di pasqua*. Then there is the whole *colombe* thing (the Easter version of *pannetone*). And I guess some people actually do go to Mass, since

Easter is a religious holiday and not just an excuse for a big meal.

But me? This is the time of year when I order my *abbacchio*, or "baby lamb," to roast in our wood-fueled oven up in Todi. While I usually get a rosemary-garlic thing going, some years I experiment and turn to Morocco and France for inspiration.

But what I really love about Easter is not the lame gift that usually comes inside the big hollow Easter eggs. I like the gift that comes inside the little lamb: coratella.

Coratella is the Italian word for "lamb's pluck." Not that you've ever heard of that word before, I'm sure. Lamb's pluck is the lungs, liver, and heart of a lamb, all still connected by the esophagus. It's not an easy cut of meat to find, and is somewhat seasonal since it's best when it comes from freshly slaughtered young spring lambs: abbacchio.

The recipe I use is the one I've been using ever since I discovered my first coratella hiding inside my Easter lamb. Spring lamb coincides with spring artichokes, and nowhere do they get any better than in the area around Rome. So it was Ada Boni's *Coratella con Carciofi*, from *Il Talismano della Felicita* (the Italian equivalent of the *Joy of Cooking*). This was the tome I turned to when I first found myself with coratella in the kitchen. Ada told me how to cut up the different organs, and in which order to add them to the pan.

coratella di abbacchio con carciofi

Serves 6

(Adapted from Ada Boni's *Il Talismano della Felicita*.)

2 pounds (1 kilo) coratella, or lamb's pluck

10 artichokes

¼ cup (60 milliliters) extra-virgin
  olive oil

Salt

Freshly ground black pepper

1 onion, chopped

⅔ cup (160 milliliters) dry white wine

Chopped fresh mint leaves,
  about ½ cup

A squeeze of fresh lemon juice

Separate the organs from the connecting tissue. Cut each one into ¼-inch slices, and keep separate.

Clean, trim, and slice the artichokes into wedges. (See "All About Artichokes," page 55.)

In a large pan over medium heat, warm the olive oil. Add the artichokes and cook until tender, adding a bit of water if they dry out. Season with salt and pepper

Once the artichokes are done, in a pan large enough to hold all the innards and artichokes, heat oil over medium heat. Add the chopped onion and cook just until the onion softens a bit.

Add the lungs and cook with the onion

(this way the onion won't overcook), adding a bit of water if the onion starts to brown. Let the lungs cook until they are browned and give off their characteristic whistle, 15 to 20 minutes.

Season with salt and pepper, and add about ⅓ cup of the white wine. Let it evaporate and add the heart. After 2 minutes, add the liver and let it cook for another minute or two. Once the liver has lost its rosy color, add the artichokes. Stir and add the remaining ⅓ cup wine. Let it cook a bit more and add the chopped mint.

Transfer the coratella to a platter and squeeze some lemon juice over the top. Coratella should be served piping hot. I like to serve it with mashed potatoes.

eating other animals

When I first met Domenico and started dating him I was living in Florence and he was living in Rome. I would come down almost every weekend to visit him. While I knew Rome very well, he was living in Monti, an area I had only been to once to visit a church designed by Giacomo della Porta. Centrally located and tucked into an area between the Roman Forum and the Colosseum, it is one of the city's oldest neighborhoods. It had always been known as a kind of rough neighborhood, far from the borderline hipster, downright trendy place it is today.

When Domenico first moved into the flat, most of the "hotels" down the street were full of rooms that were rented by the hour by the working ladies, and the owner of Domenico's flat—an old woman—had kept chickens on the rooftop terrace.

One day as I was looking out the living room window, at the building across the street, I saw the outlines of lettering that seemed like it had only been taken down recently. As I tried to make out the word, I must have been talking out loud, since Domenico said, "Oh yeah, that was the horse butcher. They closed six months ago."

While Domenico didn't grow up eating horse, he didn't understand my shock at the prospect. In Italy, until quite recently, horse was thought of as a particularly iron-rich meat that was fed to the sick and the infirm to give them strength. It was also pretty much of a delicacy, and not only for sale at most butchers' but also, as Domenico had pointed out, there were entire butcher shops that specialized in it.

These days most of the equine butchers in Rome have closed shop (there are two left in Testaccio), but that doesn't mean I don't expand my cooking to include other animals that I didn't grow up eating.

One of my favorites is rabbit. I guess since I never had a pet rabbit, I don't really have any "bunny" issues. Also, in this day and age of battery hens full of antibiotics and god knows what else, you can always be pretty sure the rabbit you buy is raised humanely and, hopefully, not shot up with additives.

rabbit vignarola

Serves 6

Vignarola, a spring stew made up of artichokes, peas, and fava beans, is a Roman specialty. A recent trend in Roman restaurants is to make vignarola as part of another dish. I think that one of the main reasons most restaurants hesitate to add vignarola on its own to the menu is that they don't know quite where to put it. First course? Side dish? Antipasto? It is any and all of the above. To resolve this issue restaurants like Cesare and Taverna dei Fori Imperiali have been using vignarola as a pasta sauce. Brilliant, right?

But I decided to delve into the unchartered second course arena. I had a beautifully boned rabbit from the farmers' market, so I used that as the base. I browned the rabbit first, then pretty much proceeded with the vignarola as I normally would. But with one big exception.

I waited until the very last minute to add big handfuls of chopped scallions, spring garlic, parsley, and lemon zest. And the peas were the last to go in. Tender and sweet, they needed only about 2 minutes of cooking before I

was able to bring the dish to the table. And while this stew is never going to win any beauty awards, at least I finally accomplished what I'd always wanted to do: make a vignarola that looked as springy and vibrant as I knew it tasted.

If you can't find rabbit, and I know this can be difficult, then substitute chicken. But please use a mixture of breast and thighs, or even all thighs, if possible.

> 2 tablespoons extra-virgin olive oil
> One 3-pound (1½ kilos) rabbit, cut into 2-inch pieces
> Salt
> Freshly ground black pepper
> 6 artichokes, trimmed and cut into wedges (see "All About Artichokes," page 55)
> 1 cup freshly shelled fava beans
> 1 cup (250 milliliters) dry white wine
> 4 scallions, chopped
> 4 fresh spring garlic bulbs, chopped
> 2 cups freshly shelled peas
> ½ cup chopped fresh flat-leaf parsley
> Zest of 1 lemon, roughly chopped
> 3 tablespoons fresh lemon juice

In a sauté pan large enough to hold everything, add the oil and place over high heat. Add the rabbit and brown well, seasoning with salt and pepper. Once the rabbit is browned, stir in the artichokes and fava beans. Add the white wine, scraping up the browned bits from the bottom of the pan. Cover and let simmer over low heat for about 25 minutes. Check every now and then and add some water if it looks too dry.

Once the rabbit and artichokes are tender, add the scallions, garlic, and peas. Stir, cover, and cook for about 1 minute. Test to make sure the peas are done. Turn off the heat; add the parsley, lemon zest, and lemon juice. Stir, taste, and adjust the seasoning if needed. Serve immediately while peas are still pretty and green.

If you are going to prepare this ahead, wait until you reheat it to add the final five ingredients.

where to eat offal in rome

Checchino dal 1887

Via di Monte Testaccio 30, 39-06-574-3816

➤ This is one of the oldest restaurants in Testaccio, and certainly the fanciest, which offers some of the best traditional offal in Rome. Don't miss their *insalata di zampi,* an old-fashioned salad made of veal trotter, boned and tossed with a tepid mix of celery, carrots, and beans and dressed with salsa verde. The dish I would gladly eat every day is the *rigatoni alla pajata.* Again, while most Testaccio restaurants do serve this, I rarely order it since it usually comes with a few measly squiggles of intestine thrown into a tomato sauce. Checchino does it right, with the ratio of rigatoni to pajata being about 50:50. The sauce tastes like pajata, just like it should, with a healthy dusting of sharp pecorino.

Their best dish, though, is the mixed grill of pajata, kidney, sweetbreads, and liver—all crispy, crunchy, salty, and cooked just until barely done.

Armando al Pantheon

Salita dei Crescenzi 31, 39-06-6880-3034

➤ This old-school trattoria near the Pantheon almost always has at least some offal on the menu, which changes daily. Their Roman-style stewed tripe (made with wild mint) is heavenly, as is their antipasto of crispy grilled pajata.

Perilli

Via Marmorata 39, 39-06-575-5100

➤ My favorite restaurant in Testaccio is Perilli. My favorite main dish there is coratella, and I order it every time I see it on the menu, which is usually only in the spring. Their tripe is also excellent, and they are one of the few places left that still makes pasta served with coda alla vaccinara, "stewed oxtail."

trattoria behavior

People think that just because I write about food I get to eat in fancy restaurants all the time. Far from it. First of all, fancy restaurants are expensive and I usually pay for my meals. And second, I naturally tend toward the simpler end of the eatery spectrum. Especially in Italy.

Up until recently, when you wanted to go out to eat in Rome the landscape was very strictly defined. At the upper end of things there were *ristoranti*. White tablecloths on tables, ancient waiters (never waitresses) in white jackets, and a menu from which you were expected to order at least two courses. Prices were relatively high, and you were paying as much for the formal setting and service as for the food itself.

At the other end of the spectrum there were the *osteria* and *trattoria*. These simpler places started out life as places that sold wine. This was where laborers could come with their own food—a piece of bread, an onion, and maybe a hunk of cheese—sit down, and order a carafe of white Frascati. Eventually these places started serving food as well: simple pastas and maybe one or two main courses. And always: wine by the carafe.

When I lived in Rome in the '70s, when heading out to eat we gravitated to the trattorie. Cheap as could be, I remember clearly that a plate of pasta was usually about 600 lire (about 60 cents). Ristoranti—like Piperno or La Campana—were reserved for special occasions like birthdays or grandparents visiting. But it was to the corner trattoria that we headed for weekend dinners or any night my mother didn't feel like cooking.

One of my favorite parts of eating in these trattorie was the wine dispensers. Massive, refrigerated cabinets took up the entire back wall. They were usually fronted with a mirror etched with a Roman scene or a still life of grapes. But the main action was the little spigots. This is where the waiter would hold a hastily rinsed, stocky glass carafe and fill it up to the top with slightly fizzy white wine. The wine was straw colored and the still active fermentation would not only result in a foamy head, but also a heady, almost sour, distinctly wine smell that I would forever associate with eating out in Rome.

Although I wasn't old enough to drink, I was completely fascinated by the entire procedure. I loved the bow-waisted glass carafes as well as the short chunky glasses that were used to drink wine, water, or, more commonly, a mixture of both. I was completely mystified how the wine came out of the faucets, just like water. It was one of the sure signs that, in fact, Italy was a lot different than where I had grown up in St. Louis, where faucets were for water. I actually thought that wine was part of the plumbing. It wasn't until much later that I realized that large trucks were coming in from Frascati and piping in barrel loads of wine directly into large vats.

Although these trattorie and osterie were simple, that didn't mean they were without their own unwritten codes. My sisters and I soon learned the rules that every Roman already knew. There were certain things you ordered at specific places, and even certain dishes that were only available on specific days of the week. We took to going out on Thursdays since my sister Jodi was obsessed with gnocchi and this was the day they were served. You would never think of ordering fish on a Sunday or Monday (no boats go out on those days), but on Friday you wouldn't order anything but fish.

At the same time there were things on the menu that no person would ever order. *Insalata Russa*, a mixture of boiled vegetables, pickles, and mayonnaise, was, at the time, on almost all menus. But it was something that no one I knew ever ordered, anywhere.

Another thing my sisters and I were fascinated with was the display of antipasti that would greet us when we walked in the door. Almost every trattoria we went to had a display of platters filled with gleaming, colorful choices: thick slices of bright yellow *frittata*, glistening orbs of sweet and sour onions, parsley-flecked seafood salad, and too many kinds of roasted vegetables and salads to name. This abundant display would change with the seasons, including artichokes in the spring and platters full of tangled wild greens in the winter.

The location of the antipasto display was crucial. Since you were forced to pass by the display as you made your way to your table, this almost guaranteed that you would order something, even if it was only a small dish of marinated black olives. The smells and sights were just too tantalizing to pass up.

In recent years this type of antipasto display seems to be a dying breed. I think it may be partly due to health regulations (I'm not sure platters of room-temperature food within easy reach of everyone walking by comply with current EU norms), but I also suspect it has to do a bit with changing eating habits. *Antipasto* translates as "before the meal," and these days, with people watching what they eat as well as what they spend, it's a rare case that you would order three full courses in any restaurant. The antipasto course has sadly been a casualty of these trends.

Luckily there are still a few very old-fashioned places that choose to stick to tradition. Nerone, a nothing-special kind of place, is one of my favorites. While one of the main attractions of this neighborhood tratorria is the rickety tables with direct views of the Colosseum, locals come here for the massive antipasto counter in the back. Adapting to current regulations, the owners have installed a long, refrigerated display case that runs almost the length of the room. Glass shelves balance white platters filled with all of my favorites. Like all good antipasto spreads, it is heavy on the vegetables: grilled and marinated peppers, stewed artichokes, and breaded and fried eggplant. Then there are the *fritti:* small balls of rice, potato croquettes, and breaded stuffed olives, orbs of pure white mozzarella, black and green marinated olives, and at least three kinds of seafood salad.

my five favorite trattorie

These days true trattorie are a dying breed. I'm talking about humble, paper-covered-table kind of places. Here are a few that are left.

Sora Margherita

Piazza delle Cinque Scole 30, 39-06-687-4216
➤ Sora Margherita is, literally, a hole in the wall. Its fifteen paper-topped tables are crammed into a long narrow space that barely has room for a kitchen. Get there by 12:15 and put your name on the waiting list. Then sit on one of the chairs outside and wait. It's worth it. Trust me. (They start serving at 12:30.) Don't miss: deep-fried artichokes and cacio e pepe con ricotta.

Settimio

Via del Pellegrino 117, 39-06-688-01978
➤ Simple, bare-bones trattoria. The kitchen is the size of a closet, but manages to turn out Roman classics, including freshly made pasta. Nothing fancy. No whole grilled sea bass or grouper here. This is what keeps the prices pretty low; that and the other lovingly prepared standards, served on thick white plates, no garnish.

Don't be put off by the locked door; they are, indeed open, if they decide to let you in.

Enoteca Corsi

Via del Gesu 87/88, 39-06-679-0821, lunch only

➢ An old-fashioned "bottle" shop, selling wine in the front room—the real action is in back. Paper-topped tables and wooden chairs are all original. A daily menu is thrown on the table, outlining the dozen specials of the day. Everything is rough, ready, and delicious.

Dar Filettaro

Largo dei Librari 88, 39-06-686-4018, dinner only

➢ This small hole-in-the-wall doesn't kid around. They serve one thing, and one thing only: big, steaming hunks of freshly fried. *baccalà.* If you want to be really Roman, order a plate of *acciughe con burro,* anchovies with butter. But the main draw is of course the baccalà.

Tonino

Via del Governo Vecchio 18–19, 333-587-0779

➢ The official name is Trattoria Antonio Bassetti, but there's barely a sign outside, and everyone just calls it Tonino's. Even though it's just down the street from the touristy Piazza Navona, you'll find more regulars here than tourists. The space is cramped, tables are draped in cheery checked cloth, and the menu never changes. This is the place to order bucatini all'amatriciana, gnocchi (on Thursdays), or spaghetti alla gricia. Seconds usually include stuffed zucchini, meatballs, and—on Fridays—baccalà.

places that still have an antipasto buffet

Nerone

Via delle Terme di Tito 96, 39-06-481-7952

➢ Nerone has one of the few old-fashioned big antipasto spreads left. I'll say right up front, there isn't any grand innovation or creativity here. What there is are seasonal vegetables, cooked in a few different ways, served without fanfare. Grilled peppers simply dressed with oil and a bit of garlic; fried eggplant, breaded and drizzled with a light tomato sauce; pan-fried zucchini rounds dressed with vinegar and mint; artichokes, stewed until they become like silk.

Hosteria L'Orso 80

Via del'Orso 33, 39-06-686-4904

➢ The main reason to go to this large and old-fashioned place just a block from Piazza Navona is the antipasto spread. Have a seat and just say the word *antipasti* and sit back for the ride. The plates start coming and don't really stop until the waiters can't find any more space on the table. The small plates include a bit of everything: small veal meatballs in tomato sauce, focaccia, mozzarella, fried zucchini flowers, prosciutto and melon, grilled vegetables, beans, seafood salad. The rest of the menu is excellent, but it's the antipasto that's the thing. And you may very well be too full to carry on.

Costanza

Piazza del Paradiso 63, 39-06-686-1717

➤ Costanza is more restaurant than trattoria, but still continues the tradition of displaying antipasti in the entranceway. Platters of artichokes, roasted peppers, and stuffed zucchini nudge up against seafood salad and marinated octopus.

when in rome . . . trattoria rules

1. *What to order?:* Almost no one is expected to order three full courses anymore. Two courses will do just fine. An antipasto and a first or second course or else a pasta and a main dish are enough.

2. *Splitting a dish:* You can do it, but remember, portions in Italy are smaller than in the States.

3. *Tipping:* Take a look at your bill. If there is a charge for service, then just a few euros left on the table will suffice. If service is not included, then 10 percent is standard.

4. *Bread:* The bread basket is not a free antipasto course. The bread is there to be eaten with either your antipasto, main dish, or salad. Italians do not ask

for a dish of olive oil and then proceed to eat the basketful of bread before the meal even starts.

recipes: roman trattoria food

celery and cheese antipasto

Serves 4

Old-fashioned Roman trattorie are quirky things. I often hear from visitors to Rome that they've looked at the menu, chosen something, only to see everyone else around them eating completely different dishes than were listed.

Not only are daily specials not listed, but also certain things, like antipasti and side dishes (contorni), remain completely mysterious. Even restaurants that I have been going to for years have special dishes that continue to escape my notice. For instance, we've been going to Perilli for Sunday lunches for about fifteen years now. And it was only last year that I discovered their delicious and, as far as I can figure out, totally unique celery and cheese antipasto. The only way we found out about it was thanks to our favorite waiter, Valerio. One afternoon Domenico and I had arrived at 1:00 to meet Sophie and Emma for lunch. For some reason (drying their hair? putting on makeup?) they were very late. Valerio took pity on us, and

(continued)

brought us over a plate of what at first glance looked to be cheese in oil.

Instead it was Perilli's amazing celery and fontina antipasto in mustard vinaigrette. Who knew? Well, I should have. It had always been available on the antipasto table for as long as we'd been going there. Tucked right between the carciofi alla romana and the stuffed zucchini. But, somehow, it had never been offered, and so it had never been ordered. It's now become one of our favorite dishes. The white tender celery hearts are cut into long sticks, as is the fontina. They are then mixed together with a lemony vinaigrette made with mustard. Not spicy French Dijon mustard, but a more mild and fruity one, basically any supermarket mustard that you can get in Italy (more French's than Grey Poupon).

4 to 5 celery heart stalks (only the whitest inner stalks)
¼ pound (150 grams) fontina cheese (see note)
1½ tablespoons yellow prepared mustard, such as French's
⅓ cup extra-virgin olive oil
3 tablespoons fresh lemon juice
Salt
Freshly ground black pepper
Crusty Italian bread, for serving

Cut the celery stalks into 3-inch-long, thickish pieces. Cut the cheese into the same shape.

Put the mustard into a small bowl. Slowly drizzle in the olive oil, a bit at a time, stirring to emulsify the mixture, then pour in more; it will get very thick. Slowly add the lemon juice and taste. If you like it more lemony, add more lemon juice. Season with salt and pepper to taste.

Combine everything in a bowl and mix well. Let sit for at least an hour before serving. This allows the cheese to absorb the flavors of the vinaigrette and the celery to wilt just a bit.

Place the antipasto in a small, shallow serving dish, set in the center of the table, and let everyone serve themselves. Accompany with bread, and soon you'll see everyone fighting to dip their bread in the leftover dressing.

Note: If you can't get fontina, then a high-quality Swiss would work just fine.

cacio e pepe

Serves 4–5

More or less the Roman version of macaroni and cheese, it's a poor man's dish, involving nothing more than three ingredients. While it was always available in the simplest of trattorie, this was not a dish that was common in the general restaurant scene in Rome until about fifteen years ago, when it was "rediscovered." Now every chef worth his while is experimenting with different fancied-up versions. Although one of the most typical shapes of pasta to use is fresh *tonnarelli*, I find that packaged rigatoni is easier to handle at home.

Although the recipe seems easy, it's not. Make sure you follow the directions about the stirring and adding of cheese, or else you will end up with a big, ugly clump.

> 1 pound (500 grams) rigatoni
> 4 ounces (120 grams) young pecorino cheese, grated
> 2 to 3 tablespoons freshly ground black pepper

Bring a large pot of salted water to a boil. Add the pasta and cook until al dente.

Meanwhile, mix the grated cheese with the pepper and set aside. Make sure your pasta bowl is heated, or else your cheese will clump up. You can heat the bowl by letting it sit with hot water in it until you are ready to use it.

When the pasta is done, drain it, reserving 1 cup of the pasta cooking water. Transfer the pasta to the large heated bowl. Add handfuls of cheese to the pasta, mixing as you go, and alternating with a bit of the reserved pasta cooking water so it doesn't get dried out. Keep doing this until you have used all the cheese. You want to add the cheese slowly so it doesn't all melt and clump up, but don't overstir, or again, it will all come together in a clump.

Grind a bit more black pepper on top, and serve immediately. In fact, most trattorie tend to do the mixing at the table.

Variation: Sora Margherita serves their cacio e pepe with a big, heaping dollop of fresh ricotta atop each plate. Not traditional at all, but absolutely divine.

{ chapter 14 }

how to feed a roman dog and raise a roman baby

One of the first conversations that I ever had with Domenico concerned our future dog, Chester. We were on our first date in Florence, and little did I know that almost everything about that evening would predict the rest of my life. For our very first date Domenico showed up forty-five minutes late. Twenty-five years later, he has still not mastered the art of being on time. Even though Domenico had invited me on this date, once he showed up, I found out he had no idea where to go for dinner and hadn't made any reservations. Twenty-five years later, not only am I fully in charge of our dinner plans, but I have actually made a career out of it.

So it really shouldn't be surprising that since much of our talk that night was about Jack Russells, we would end up with one very bad, but dearly loved, Jack Russell that would take over our lives for the following fourteen years. Over dinner at Acqua al Due (my choice) Domenico and I found out we had much in common. Various friends in the art world, architectural historians we both knew (some of whom were disconcertingly his ex-girlfriends), and, weirdly, our shared obsession with Jack Russells.

This was way before Jack Russells became the dog du jour for anyone who owned a leash. Where did our passion come from? Where any New York–centric person gets his or her prepackaged passion: *The New Yorker*. As it turned out we had both read the same article about Brian Plummer and his rat-catching dogs. It was a good old-fashioned *New Yorker* article, at least fifteen pages long. By the end of it, we were both dreaming of our own little black-and-white puppy, even if we didn't have any rats to catch. So, really, it seemed like fate that we should meet each other and fall in love so that we could bring our Jack Russell dream to fruition. Right then and there, over dessert, we even named him: Chester, after a much-loved bird I had had to leave behind in New York when I moved to Florence.

So a few short months later, I surprised Domenico with a beribboned Chester. Only two months old, he was immediately a nightmare. Cute, but a nightmare. He had a cough. He had a limp. He tried to bite just about everyone. But we loved him, because he was our first baby.

And like any baby, I had to feed him. There was a small store down the street from me in Florence that seemed to sell everything, so I headed there bright and early to pick up some dog food. Having never owned a dog before, I was pretty sure I would have a choice of either canned food or dry, and was prepared to buy a bit of both just to be on the safe side.

So I was really confused that the shop owner responded to my request of *"Cibo per cane, per favore"* ("Dog food, please") with the response *"Riso o pasta?"* ("Rice or pasta?"). No, no, I tried to explain to him, I wanted dog food, not human food. At which point he just gave up trying to communicate with this obviously confused foreigner and just pointed over to two big bins that I'd never noticed before. One was full of broken pasta, and the other of rice. And that's when it dawned on me: I was going to have to cook for my dog.

At which point just about everyone else in the shop chimed in. One lady clutching a small trembling Yorkie told me that "Danilo was a bit under the weather today, so he just had a bit of rice in chicken broth." While a man buying 10 kilos of the broken pasta let me know he just mixes this up with leftover table scraps for his German shepherd. *"Blackie mangia tutto!"* ("Blackie eats everything!")

I was going to have to cook for Chester? Every day? And adjust his diet according to how he was feeling? Thinking that this was a bit more than I had bargained for, I finally spied a few dusty cans of Ciappi sitting on the shelf. Since the labels pictured a smiling and very healthy-looking golden retriever, I figured this was my answer. As I went to take two cans everyone in the shop once again chimed in, *"Ma che schifezza!"* ("How disgusting!") It turns out that no self-respecting Italian dog owner would ever think of feeding their dog canned food. I mean really, would you eat canned food yourself?

And so I cooked for Chester. Rice with a bit of egg. Pasta with butter and cheese. He seemed very happy with his meals.

But Chester's catered dinners soon came to an end. By the time he was one year old, I was expecting Sophie and there was no way I was going to deal with preparing meals for two very needy little creatures. So Chester was weaned onto cans of Ciappi, while my education on feeding an Italian child began.

Oddly, my experience at the pediatrician's was not unlike my first foray into buying dog food. While I expected the doctor to let me know about various brands of baby food, I got a crash course in what Italian babies eat.

Actually, the first lesson I received about feeding Sophie was while I was still in the hospital. Over the course of the week I spent in the clinic where Sophie was born, the nurse would come in every few hours to weigh her. At first I thought that she was just hyperattentive to see if Sophie was growing. (So fast? In just one day?) But I soon realized that it was my skill and ability to feed her that was being weighed. Sophie would be plunked on a scale right before and right after she was fed. And I began to equate the nurse's attitude toward me—was she smiling? Was she disapproving?—with my ability to feed my child.

Like the folks I first ran into while buying dog food for Chester, almost everyone had an opinion about how I was supposed to be feeding Sophie. This is when I first learned the word *minestrina*. Even people who don't speak Italian know the word *minestrone*, a hearty, often chunky Italian vegetable soup. But when the pediatrician told me that one of the first things I could feed Sophie was minestrina, I had no idea what he was talking about. Since *-ina* added to anything makes it a diminutive, I thought he was referring to the portion size. And while Sophie would be starting out with pint-size portions of anything, the *-ina* in this case meant just a lighter version of what Domenico and I were already eating.

I was supposed to make a special soup, with a cut-up carrot, a piece of celery, and maybe a potato. Not too much salt, *per favore*. Then strain this, and the resulting vegetable broth would be Sophie's first foray into the wide world of adult food. When I mentioned that this sounded kind of unappetizing, that I doubted a weak vegetable broth would be very appealing, he responded: "Not once you add the grated Parmesan cheese and olive oil."

And that's when I realized that as far as feeding children here in Italy there was to be none of the special "kids" food, but just versions of what the adults (and dogs, I guess) already knew and loved. So after Sophie showed no problem enjoying her first bowls of minestrina, I was allowed to add the next step: *pastina*. Yes, itty-bitty pieces of pasta made just for babies, with loads of olive oil and freshly grated Parmesan cheese.

Like most Italian children, Sophie and Emma thus never had to make any transition from "children's food" like fish fingers and chicken nuggets. They pretty much did what most kids here do: eat what their parents are eating. This meant that they soon left behind watered-down vegetable soup and were ordering tripe and liver whenever they got the chance and digging into freshly caught sea urchins along the *lungomare* in Puglia.

recipes

Even though Italian children eat pretty much what adults eat, there are certain foods that kids here know and love and associate with their childhood. The dishes change from region to region, and even from family to family. The following are pretty standard, and were, and still are, Sophie's and Emma's favorites.

pasta con burro

Serves 5

You would think this would be a no-brainer. Pasta with butter should just always be pasta with butter, right? But I got a very big shock one day, when Sophie and Emma were little, when I served them what I thought was one of their favorite dishes. "It's doesn't taste like Sandra's." Translation: "Sandra's tastes better than yours." Sandra is our neighbor in Umbria, and the girls would spend mornings there during the summer while I worked.

The next time I dropped off Sophie and Emma I made a point to ask Sandra for her secret recipe. As it turned out not only did she use unsalted butter (I had been using fancy imported salted butter from Denmark), but she also added one secret ingredient: the pasta cooking water. Evidently this trick emulsified the butter into a starchy sauce that made Sandra's so much better. Also? Sandra always used spaghetti, never penne. This, too (according to Sophie and Emma), made all the difference. As Sandra explained to me, "Signora, children prefer *spaghetti*," as if it was something everyone knew. And the final touch, a drizzle of olive oil, made it irresistible.

Salt
1 pound (500 grams) spaghetti
4 tablespoons (½ stick/60 grams)
    unsalted butter, at room temperature,
    cut into small pieces
Extra-virgin olive oil

Bring a pot of salted water to a boil. Add the spaghetti and cook until al dente.

Drain the pasta, reserving a cup of the pasta cooking water. Return the pasta to the warm pot and add the butter. Stir in the butter, so that it begins to melt, adding the pasta cooking water a bit at a time, and continuing to stir. A buttery, starchy sauce should form.

Serve with a bit of olive oil drizzled on top. Or, better yet, let your children drizzle their own oil, which is part of the fun.

pasta with butter and anchovies

Serves 4

Pasta con burro is definitely comfort food. While delicious and almost everyone's secret vice, it's not really something that you would serve to guests, right? But with just a couple of tweaks this homey dish can become dinner party fare.

I started thinking about this because pasta with butter is currently enjoying quite a vogue in Rome in restaurants. But it's not your everyday pasta with butter. Pasta with butter and the all-important addition of anchovies has become something every new restaurant is putting on its menu. In fact, you'd think that there was some sort of new law that required it as a prerequisite to opening a restaurant. It's definitely a trend, but at least an incredibly delicious one.

It is beyond easy to make in the comfort of your own home, even if you're far from the *centro storico*. The trick, of course, is making the effort to source the right ingredients. Freshly made egg pasta to start, then the very best anchovies money can buy. Big fat fillets packed in oil are my favorite, preferably from Sicily or, if I'm feeling particularly flush, imported anchovies from the northern coast of Spain.

And butter—lots of butter. And no one in his right mind would use Italian butter for this dish. Italians are good at lots of things, but butter is not one of them. I usually opt for imported Danish butter, but the best was when I happened to have a pack of French butter Sophie had received as a Christmas present from her boss (good bosses give good butter), which made all the difference.

Once you've got your ingredients, the rest is pretty simple, but not as straightforward as you might think. I use anchovies twice: first dissolved into the melted butter, and then a few thick fillets added at the last minute. And to achieve the most luscious of sauces, you must make ample use of the starchy pasta cooking water. When everything is placed in a warmed bowl and topped with a few grindings of black pepper, you can pretend you're in one of Rome's trendiest restaurants. Or just call it what it is: comfort food. Your choice.

Salt

8 tablespoons (1 stick/110 grams) good-quality unsalted butter

12 anchovy fillets

1 pound (500 grams) fresh fettuccine

Freshly ground black pepper

Bring a large pot of salted water to a boil.

Put three-quarters (6 tablespoons) of the butter into a pan large enough to hold the cooked and drained pasta, and melt over medium heat. Add half of the anchovies and stir until they have dissolved.

(continued)

Once the water is boiling, add the pasta and cook until al dente. If it is fresh pasta it will cook very quickly, so keep your eye on it

Drain the pasta, reserving a cup of the pasta cooking water. Transfer the drained pasta to the pan with the butter and toss well to coat over medium heat.

Add about ¼ cup of the pasta cooking water, and stir well. Turn off the heat and add the remaining 2 tablespoons butter and a bit more of the pasta cooking water, stirring to amalgamate.

Add the remaining anchovies, toss, and serve immediately. Season with the pepper.

Note: For a boost of "anchoviness," use *colatura,* a reduced anchovy liquid from Campania, in addition to the anchovies.

zabaione

Serves 2

One of my husband's iconic childhood food memories is zabaione. His fondest memories are when he arrived home from school and his mother would make him a special treat. Taking out a big bowl and a large fork (she didn't own a whisk), his mother would whip him up a fresh batch of this homey custard.

We've had more fights than I can tell you about this. First of all, when Sophie and Emma were little, he would encourage me to make it for them. When I balked at feeding a one-year-old raw eggs, his response was "It didn't hurt me!" I also have an issue with his referring to this as zabaione at all, since traditional zabaione includes at least some sweet dessert wine, which I know his mother would never have included. As it turns out, we are both right. There is a version of this traditional recipe, for children, that eliminates the wine. The resulting dessert is completely different, but delicious just the same. And while Domenico insists his mother never got hers anywhere near the heat, just whipping up an egg yolk with sugar, I prefer to cook it over a bain-marie. A dash of vanilla replaces the flavoring of the Marsala.

4 egg yolks
⅓ cup (80 grams) sugar
¼ cup (250 milliliters) heavy cream
¼ teaspoon pure vanilla extract

Place all the ingredients in a metal bowl; select a bowl that will later fit over a pan of simmering water.

Using an electric mixer or a whisk, beat until the mixture is light and frothy; it should be very light in color. Place the bowl over a pan of barely simmering water and continue whisking for another 10 minutes. It will continue to expand and become even creamier.

You can either eat it immediately, warm, or place it in small single-serving cups and chill in the refrigerator, where it will become firmer.

to panino or not to panino? that is the roman question

Remember when everyone was getting those panino presses? I think it was about fifteen years ago, when the hot item in every fancy cooking supply catalogue was a machine whose sole purpose was to take an Italian-style sandwich and press it down between two heated steel plates until the outside was crisp and the inside was warm and (since we are talking America here) probably oozing with melted cheese.

The investment was worth it—or so it was implied—so that you could have an authentic Italian panino in the comfort of your own home.

The main problem with this is that no Italian ever thinks of having a panino in the comfort of their own home. Panini (and we'll get into what that means specifically in Rome) are meant to be eaten only in situations where a full sit-down meal is not possible or convenient. Going to the beach? Pack a panino. Train ride? Panino. Hungry for a quick lunch on a short work break? Panino from your local coffee bar.

I realized this cultural divide during one of our yearly trips to the States. When we head back home, we usually spend a week at my sister Robin's house. Like all good moms, she always has a loaf of bread, some cold cuts, and a jar of pickles in the fridge. When lunchtime rolls around, everything is laid out on the counter and it is more or less fend for yourself.

Taking pity on my Italian husband, I made a sandwich for him. Two slices of rye bread, some corned beef, Swiss cheese, mayo, and mustard. While he enjoyed it, I knew, from the shaking of his head, that this was a very strange thing to be calling a real meal.

Back in Rome, I tried to introduce the idea of a sandwich for a meal. Even when I went out of my way to get great bread, interesting cheeses and prosciutto, and fresh lettuce leaves for a sandwich all made to order and put on a plate with a side of cut carrots, pickles, and even homemade coleslaw, my family was having none of this. I'm not sure how my 50 percent American daughters decided that they were 100 percent Italian when it came to meals. Even if I was putting it on a plate, which was sitting on a tablecloth in our dining room, a panino was just not going to be a real meal.

It wasn't until Sophie headed off to middle school that she began to appreciate my oh-so-American sandwich-making skills. Since it was a long day before she came home for lunch at 2:00 p.m., she would get famished. To avoid the inevitable drops in blood sugar, I started slipping an aluminum foil–wrapped sandwich into the outside pocket of her backpack. Her first reaction was, of course, one of embarrassment. While any fourteen-year-old will be embarrassed by almost anything their mother does, I think the thought of pulling out an obviously "American snack," made by her mother was just too horrific to contemplate.

Until, that is, she started asking me if I could possibly make two . . . and then three.

At first I thought that she was just going through a growth spurt. But I quickly realized that her sandwiches not only had become an object of curiosity in her class, but were beginning to become requested by her schoolmates. In fact, I found out my sandwiches had a name: *panini di Litzie.*

What made my little panini such objects of desire? It sure wasn't artisan bread and raw milk cheese. For Sophie's snacks I pulled out a loaf of industrially made Mulino Bianco bread, slapped on store-bought turkey breast, a leaf of lettuce, and copious amounts of my favorite brand of Italian mayonnaise, Calve. This, of course, made them completely exotic and exciting. They were "American" panini, and so (at least in the then-preteens' eyes) so much better than the typical Roman *panini* they were used to. Which is all kind of ironic since, of course, true Roman panini are (at least in my foodie adult eyes) so much better.

Like many Italian food words, *panino* is a loaded one. From region to region the definition slips from one thing to another. In Palermo soft rolls are layered with spleen, while in Florence mobile carts serve up steaming spoonfuls of tripe onto crusty ciabatta. In Venice soft white bread is cut into triangles and stuffed with things like chicken salad, tiny shrimp, or simple ham, all with copious amounts of mayonnaise to become *tramezzini.*

anatomy of a roman panino: the bread

Rosetta. For a long time the rosetta roll held sway over every other kind of bread used to make a panino. When I lived here in the '70s, it was just about the only bread you'd see. It was what showed up in bread baskets in restaurants and was certainly what every school kid looked forward to at lunch. The rosetta is made by laying five small balls of dough next to each other in a circle, with a sixth ball stuck on top in the center. After it has been left to rise, it is baked in a hot oven where the magic occurs. While the outside becomes golden and the separation between the balls becomes a lovely rose-shaped pattern (get it? rosetta?), the inside puffs up and is completely hollow, which makes it the perfect vehicle for a panino.

Tartaruga. A cousin of the rosetta, the tartaruga has a flat shape and crisscrossing pattern that make it look like a turtle. I guess.

Pizza Bianca. One of my all-time favorite Roman sandwiches is the pizza bianca type. The Roman panino par excellence is *pizza e mortazza,* or pizza bianca sliced open horizontally and layered with a slice or two of mortadella.

Ciabatta. This word *ciabatta* literally translates as "slipper," and refers to the elongated, flattish shape, which, if you really stretch your imagination, I guess looks like some sort of slipper? In any case, the word *ciabatta* changes meaning slightly from region to region, sometimes referring to a large loaf and sometimes (as here in Rome) referring to a largish roll. In Rome, ciabattas are often seasoned with a bit of olive oil on top, which makes the rustic crumb even softer and so perfect for slicing open lengthwise and turning into a panino.

Ciriola. A smallish football-shaped roll with a very sturdy crumb and crispy crust, it was traditionally the roll favored by workers, since the sturdy construction not only was filling in and of itself, but also could be amply stuffed. Ciriola are getting harder and harder to find these days.

anatomy of a roman panino: the filling

Roman sandwiches, including the rosetta, are things of minimal beauty. Three or four slices of salami. Or a few slices of mozzarella and a tomato. That's it—no quarter pound of ham, and certainly no mustard or mayonnaise. Condiments are generally frowned upon, mostly, I suppose, because they just don't form part of the Italian diet. And when you think about it,

if you've already got something as heavily seasoned as mortadella, provolone, or porchetta, do you really want or need mustard and/or mayo?

when in rome . . .

One of the most welcome trends in the Roman dining scene has been the opening of "gourmet" panino shops. While I hate to use the word *gourmet* in any context, I'm using it here since it's the word the young owners are using themselves. The trend actually was kick-started in Florence, by Alessandro Frassica and his now-famous sandwich shop 'Ino. He was one of the first to raise the humble panino to lofty heights by focusing on extraordinary quality of both bread and fillings while remaining pretty tied to Italian tradition. Here follow a few of the better of his Roman offspring:

Tricolore
Via Urbana 126

➢ Until recently Tricolore was a bit of everything. Cooking school, bread shop, and gourmet panino source. They have recently relaunched themselves and are now featuring only their much-loved gourmet panini. Not simple bread and prosciutto fare, but the best gourmet sandwiches in town: Egg and Truffle on Corn Bread; Octopus on Potato Bread; Bollito with Salsa Verde on Sourdough. Each roll is specially baked in the morning to pair with specific sandwiches.

Zia Rosetta
Via Urbana 54

➢ This adorable sandwich shop is named after the old-fashioned rosetta bread roll, which is stuffed in about fifteen different ways. Fillings are simple, yet inventive, with cute names like Lady Godiva (meatballs) and Allspice (chicken curry). Since they offer both full-size and mini panini, I like to get three small ones so I'm able to try as many as possible. They also deliver.

Trapizzino
Via Giovanni Branca 88

➢ The owner of one of Rome's best pizzerias, Sforno, opened this small shop in Testaccio, which offers the love child of pizza and panino: the *trapizzino*. Made out of a white pizza pocket, the small triangles of dough are stuffed with things like tripe, meatballs, and chicken and peppers. Kind of like a Hot Pocket, if you insist. It's an ingenious way to eat both pizza and a main course while calling it a snack ,if you ask me.

'Ino, Eataly
Piazzale XII Ottobre 1492

➢ Alessandro Frassica kick-started the gourmet panino trend in Florence at his ground-breaking 'Ino, just behind the Uffizi Gallery. He's since branched out, and has his own counter at the Eataly in Rome.

traditional panino

At the very beginning of this chapter I stressed the fact that panini are something you eat quickly, usually while at a bar. This still holds true, and almost any bar you walk into in Rome will have a selection of freshly made panini. Made in the late morning, these panini are meant to be bought and consumed within the same day. They usually sell out by 4:00 p.m.

Depending on the type of sandwich you order, your barista may ask you if you'd like it *riscaldata* ("Would you like it heated?"). And finally, this is where the infamous panino press finally makes itself known. Not in people's homes, but as a quick way to heat up the panino. Since most panini are made from either rolls or pizza bianca, both of which have a tendency to grow hard and dry fast, a quick trip to the panino press not only softens the bread, but warms it and provides an extra layer of crispy crunch.

favorite places to grab a traditional panino

Rarely do you go out of your way to grab a panino in a bar. This is something that Romans do at the spur of the moment, when they are hungry and just don't have time for a real meal. Most neighborhood bars make decent panini, so it's hard to single out one over the other. So I'll just list a few of my favorites, which are mostly my favorites because of pure convenience.

Bernasconi

Piazza Cairoli 16

➤ Though it is better known for pastries and cakes, I often head to this coffee bar for their mini sandwiches. Small, soft rolls are sliced in half and filled with salmon and marinated artichokes. These tiny bits are perfect when I'm hungry but don't want to commit to a full-fledged panino.

Caffè Perù

Via di Monserrato 46

➤ Although this coffee bar has recently been renovated and has started serving real food, I still like stopping by here for one of their well-made panini. Even though it's located in the hypertouristy area around Campo de' Fiori, the bar still attracts mostly regulars, who stop by for a quick lunchtime sandwich.

Vanni

Via Col di Lana 10

➤ Vanni is a Roman institution. While it may have started out as a coffee bar, it now includes a full-fledged pastry section and a restaurant. I'd never think of having a real meal there (the food looks kind of institutional to me), but a Sunday cappuccino with one of their well-made panini is perfect. Located in the Prati neighborhood.

Lotti

Via Sardegna 13

➤ I first discovered Lotti when Sophie was about ten and taking tennis lessons near the Villa Borghese. I would drop her off and, bad mother that I am, wander off to find a coffee and read the newspaper. (There is only so much ten-year-old tennis playing you can watch.) In my memory it was also always cold and rainy. (Why I was leaving my child to play tennis in that weather is something I've managed to forget.) Anyway, when I first stumbled upon Lotti, it immediately became "my place." At mealtimes they actually serve real food, but my favorite thing to order is a couple of their soft tramezzini, filled with hard-boiled eggs, lettuce, and just enough mayonnaise to hold it all together.

Forno Campo de' Fiori

Piazza Campo de' Fiori

➤ When you start out with great bread, you're already ahead of the game when it comes to a panino. The Forno Campo de' Fiori is one of the best bakeries in Rome, so high-quality bread goes without saying. For years people would stop by the bakery, pick up a roll or a slice of pizza bianca, and then take it across the piazza to the alimentari to have it sliced open and turned into a sandwich with a filling of their choosing. The Forno finally realized that they could be doing a great business by making their own panini and so they acquired the corner shop across the street and turned it into one of the best sandwich shops in the center. Your best bet here is to go for one of the pizza bianca–based panini. The classic, of course, is stuffed with mortadella. But in season there are such specialties as prosciutto and figs, or tomatoes and *mozzarella di bufala*. Domenico can never resist the crusty ciriolia stuffed with a fat wedge of frittata, since it reminds him of childhood trips to the beach.

recipes

panino di frittata

Makes 4 panini

Even though Domenico won't accept a panino as a substitute for a meal when we are at home, if it's packed up for a picnic, all rules fly out the window. His favorite beach-time treat exists in his memory: the *panino di frittata* his mother used to make for him to take for a day at the beach. Made with a thick slice of frittata, the rich eggy sandwich needs no other condiments.

> 1 tablespoon extra-virgin olive oil
> 1½ cups chopped onions
> Salt
> Freshly ground black pepper
> 3 large eggs
> ¼ cup grated Parmesan cheese
> 4 crusty rolls

Pour the olive oil in an 8-inch nonstick pan and place it over medium heat. Add the onions, and season with salt and pepper. Let cook until the onions have softened, about 12 minutes.

In the meantime beat the eggs and grated cheese in a small bowl.

After the onions have cooked, add them to the eggs, stir, and pour the entire mixture back into the pan. Place a lid on the pan, and cook until the eggs have set. Turn out onto a plate and let cool.

Slice the rolls in half, and place a quarter of the frittata in each roll.

prosciutto and fig panino

Makes 1 panino

Although most people know and love the divine combination of melon and prosciutto, many are unaware of the charms of pairing prosciutto with fresh figs, maybe because fresh figs are so hard to come by. But if you do have a supply, there is nothing better than the Roman practice of smashing a few of them in between two slices of pizza bianca, with a slice of prosciutto.

> One 4-inch square focaccia or
>   pizza bianca
> 2 slices prosciutto crudo
> 4 very ripe figs

Slice the focaccia or pizza bianca open lengthwise. Lay one slice of prosciutto on the bread, then place the cut-open figs on top. Cover with another slice of prosciutto and smash down with the top piece of bread, so that the figs become almost a puree.

{ chapter 16 }

cooking like mama

've pretty much grown up cooking. My favorite toy when I was younger was my Easy-Bake Oven. Mixing the little packets of powder with water that then turned into pint-sized corn muffins, brownies, and cakes was just about my favorite thing in the world. I then moved on to the real thing, following the recipe on the back of the bag of chocolate chips so that I could turn out a batch of perfect Toll House cookies by the time I was eight.

By high school, I had moved on from Rice Krispies Treats and Duncan Hines brownies. By age fifteen I had became the de facto cook in our family. My mother, who worked, would leave me her credit card and the keys to the car so that when I came home from school I could not only do the weekly grocery shopping, but then make dinner. Homework? I did go to the library, but it was to look up recipes for things like *gado-gado* and coq au vin, rather than finish that research paper on Emily Dickinson.

Throughout university, I naturally took on the role of cooking for my roommates. I would carefully plan out a week's worth of menus, then send them off to do the grocery shopping. For the rest of the week I would work my way through *The Moosewood Cookbook*, torn-out pages from *Bon Appétit,* and *Craig Claiborne's Favorites from the New York Times.* Graduate school saw me throwing dinner parties for my starving friends even when my kitchen consisted of barely more than two burners and a toaster oven in my upper West Side studio apartment.

This is all to say that by the time I was married and raising my own family in Rome I was not some novice in the kitchen. I knew how to feed both friends and family. Give me a half- full refrigerator and I could figure out something to make for dinner. Granted, this was Italy, not the States, but I had spent a good portion of my life here and so I had learned the ins and outs of being in an Italian kitchen.

And being an Italian wife? That was a new thing for me. But being an Italian daughter-in-law? That actually proved pretty easy. Maybe it is because my mother-in-law lives about 500 kilometers away from Rome, but we've always gotten along just fine. But reproducing Mama's dishes for my Italian husband? That's another story.

And it's not like I have a husband who has grown up eating only his mother's cooking. My husband is not a *mammone*, a breed of Italian male who only leaves the comforts of his mama's home when he gets married, and even after that remains tied to his mama's apron strings. No, Domenico has traveled far and wide. He's lived in the States for extended periods of time and even spent much of his early career in Africa. So he's been exposed to, and fallen in love with, food from just about everywhere but Italy.

As a new wife, I could whip up meals to re-create the escargot he'd had in Paris, the barbecued ribs he'd eaten in Kansas City, and the Wiener schnitzel he'd had in Vienna. I was even well versed in the *ribollita* he enjoyed during college days in Florence, the *amatriciana* he's learned to love in Rome, and the *spaghetti alle vongole* from time spent on the beaches of Tuscany.

But making *orecchiette con cime di rapa* just like Domenico's *pugliese* mother makes? That one threw me for a loop for the longest time. I quickly discovered that when you are cooking for an Italian male, food is pretty much divided into two categories. The first category is the food his mother made while he was a child. The second category is everything else. And if you haven't figured it out by now, the food that his mother makes? It's the best food in the world. No comparison.

I remember my first visit to Bari. We made the five-hour trip down by car, and most of the trip was taken up discussing what we were going to be eating once we arrived. Since I had never been to Puglia, and didn't know much about the foods of that region, I was intensely curious. But I had a hard time understanding some of the dishes Domenico was describing.

And let me be clear: Domenico and I speak in English. His English is so perfect you'd think he was American. And mine is pretty good, too. So it wasn't a language problem. It was a cultural one. Domenico was busy rhapsodizing about dishes that sounded, well, boring?

A plate of fava puree with boiled greens. Pasta boiled together with other boiled greens. Some kind of pizza that really wasn't a pizza made with mashed potatoes and mortadella—or not. The mortadella addition was evidently a big family issue.

Somehow, during that first trip to Bari, over the course of three days, his mother managed to make all these dishes. Because, of course, her son had asked for them and there is nothing that brings more joy to an Italian mother than cooking for her son. The food, of course, was delicious and not, I foolishly thought, that complicated to re-create. Rosa made it all seem so easy. Her kitchen stayed neat and tidy the entire time she was cooking, and the dishes seemed to appear almost miraculously with almost no effort at all. Even the most complicated of the things we ate that first weekend— orecchiette con cime di rapa—seemed like a no-brainer. I distinctly remember thinking, "Hey, this seems pretty easy. You even cook the vegetables and pasta in the same pot."

But back in my newly wedded home, for the next few months, I tried often, and failed, to re-create this typical dish. Undercooked orecchiette. Overcooked orecchiette. Broccoli that fell apart. Broccoli that tasted nothing like Mama's.

And then there was the whole thing about getting my hands on some orecchiette in the first place. This little ear-shaped pasta is very much a pugliese thing, and although you'll find orecchiette-shaped pasta in most supermarkets, they aren't anywhere near the real thing.

Real orecchiette are thick, hard, and, when cooked correctly, slightly chewy to the bite.

But today I'm happy to say that I've finally perfected my orecchiette con cime di rapa. It's only taken me twenty years, and involves driving down to Bari to shop for ingredients.

I kid you not.

I know I bang on about local, seasonal ingredients a lot. And cime di rapa are a typical example. Although you can get some version of flowering broccoli here in Lazio, it is a completely different animal from the bunches I pick up at the market in Bari. The soil, climate, and variety give the cima di rapa from Puglia a very specific, pungent, green taste that is unique. I've never quite found the exact same taste north of Naples.

So, whenever I'm in Bari, I get at least a few kilos. I also load up on orecchiette, which are handmade by housewives working out of their homes in the old part of town.

Thus—with only a 500-kilometer drive to the market between me and my dish—I can proudly produce perfect orecchiette con cime di rapa.

recipes

fava and chicory

Serves 4 as a main course

This is one of those dishes that is so simple that it's almost a nonrecipe—a puree of fava beans served with a side of boiled greens. The idea of mixing bitter greens with an earthy starch is a great one. The magic works when the bland and the bitter come together on the plate, under a liberal pour of olive oil. You might never have had this, since most restaurants tend to fuss it up, adding garlic, onions, or even bits of pancetta. But the true poetry of the dish comes in its simplicity. If you really can't abide the bitterness of chicory, you can substitute another, sweeter, green like Swiss chard.

2 cups dried split fava beans without the
    skin (not fresh fava)
1 teaspoon salt, plus more as needed
3 pounds (1⅓ kilos) chicory greens
Extra-virgin olive oil

Place the fava beans in a bowl of water and soak for 6 hours or overnight.

Drain the beans, place them in a pot, and add enough water to come about ½ inch over the top of the beans. Add 1 teaspoon of salt and bring to a simmer. Let cook, undisturbed, until the beans are mushy-tender. Don't be tempted to stir them up. You want most of the water to be absorbed, but what's not absorbed should evaporate. It's tricky. (It can take quite a long time for the beans to cook, up to an hour and a half if they are older.) By the end you should have just enough liquid in the pot to help the beans become mush.

Using a wooden spoon, only then do you stir things up, mash and mush them into a rough puree.

(Do not cook the beans ahead of time, because the fava puree tends to solidify, sort of like polenta. If you do decide to make the favas ahead of time, you'll have to thin them out with a bit more water. The consistency should be, more or less, like that of mashed potatoes.)

In the meantime, bring a large pot of salted water to a boil. Add the chicory and cook until done, about 15 minutes. The trick with cooking the chicory is to use abundant water. This will help to tame the natural bitterness of the greens.

To serve, fill each plate with half chicory and half fava puree. Drizzle with olive oil, and sprinkle with salt. Serve with crusty bread, and enjoy.

minchilli meatballs

Serves 4 to 5 as a main course

This is a recipe that my mother-in-law used to cook for Sophie and Emma when they were little. And of course, I'm sure she made it for her sons when they were children, too. The real lesson that I learned in watching my mother-in-law make these meatballs is the role that olive oil plays in so many recipes. It's not just a vehicle for softening the garlic or onion in a dish, but is one of the main ingredients that give body and texture, not to mention taste.

7 ounces (200 grams) ground pork

7 ounces (200 grams) ground beef

7 ounces (200 grams) ground veal or turkey

½ cup grated onion

½ cup bread crumbs

⅓ cup grated Parmesan cheese

¼ cup chopped fresh flat-leaf parsley

2 garlic cloves, minced

¾ teaspoon salt, plus more to season

½ teaspoon freshly ground black pepper

1 large egg

¼ cup (60 milliliters) plus 2 tablespoons extra-virgin olive oil

One 18-ounce (500-gram) can pelati (peeled whole San Marzano) tomatoes

In a large bowl, gently combine the pork, beef, veal, onion, bread crumbs, cheese, parsley, garlic, salt, pepper, egg, and the ¼ cup of olive oil. Form the mixture into about 30 small meatballs, 1½ inches in diameter.

In a large heavy-bottomed skillet, heat the remaining 2 tablespoons of olive oil over medium heat. Add the meatballs to the skillet, about 10 at a time, so as not to overcrowd. Cook, using a spoon to turn the meatballs, until they are well browned all over. Remove from the pan, set aside, and repeat the procedure to cook the rest.

Add the tomatoes to the oil in the skillet and bring to a simmer, scraping up the bits of browned meat, and season with salt. Return the meatballs, and any juices that have formed on the plate, to the skillet. Bring back to a low simmer, cover, and cook until done, about 30 minutes.

orecchiette con cime di rapa

Serves 5 to 6

2 pounds (1 kilo) trimmed cima di rapa (broccoli rabe)

4 to 6 anchovy fillets

1 pound (500 grams) orecchiette pasta

⅓ cup (120 milliliters) extra-virgin olive oil

2 garlic cloves, chopped

¼ to ½ teaspoon hot red pepper flakes

Prepare all your ingredients before you get started.

Wash and trim the greens. This took me the longest time to figure out.

(continued)

You want to make sure that you use every bit that is tender, but that is sort of subjective. Definitely preserve the flowering heads, or *cime.* Then the tender center leaves, as well as any bigger ones that seem tender. Just make sure you eliminate any really tough stems.

As for the anchovies, you can use anchovies packed in oil, ready to go, but I like the ones that are preserved in salt. This means soaking them for about 10 minutes in room-temperature water. Then carefully open them up, take out the central bones, and rinse them off. Cut them into small pieces.

Bring a large pot of salted water to a boil. Add the orecchiette, and set the timer for 5 minutes. After 5 minutes, add the broccoli rabe and bring back to a steady simmer.

In the meantime, place the oil in a skillet that will be large enough to hold all the pasta and broccoli rabe and heat gently. Add the garlic and red pepper flakes. When the garlic becomes fragrant, add the anchovies, mixing and mashing them up with a wooden spoon. Turn off the heat so the garlic doesn't brown or burn.

After the pasta has cooked for about 12 minutes total, start checking it. Orecchiette is a tricky pasta to get right. You want it to be cooked through, but still chewy. It should be cooked more al dente than other kinds of pasta.

When it is cooked, drain the pasta and broccoli in a colander, reserving a cup of the cooking water.

Turn the heat back on under the pan with the olive oil, and add the pasta and broccoli rabe to the pan. Stir and toss over low heat, so that the pasta absorbs the oil. Add a bit of the reserved cooking water if you think it's dry, but the broccoli rabe should give the dish enough moisture.

Serve, making sure you divide the broccoli rabe evenly among the dishes, since it tends to clump up.

pizza di patate

Makes one 10-inch "pizza"

This is one of my favorite dishes that I learned from my mother-in-law. It was also the one I found most confusing. I just couldn't understand why this dish, which is basically a mashed potato casserole, was called pizza. It has nothing in common with anything I think of as pizza except for the round shape of the pan it's usually baked in.

2 pounds (1 kilo) starchy potatoes

4 tablespoons (½ stick/60 grams) unsalted butter, plus more for the pan

½ cup bread crumbs for dusting

1 egg

½ cup (118 milliliters) whole milk

1 teaspoon salt

½ cup grated Parmesan cheese

1 cup ½-inch pieces fresh mozzarella

1 cup ½-inch pieces mortadella

Peel the potatoes and cut in half if large. Bring a large pot of water to a boil, add the potatoes, and cook until tender yet firm. Drain and place in a bowl. Let cool a bit.

Preheat the oven to 350°F (180°C). Butter a 10-inch springform pan and coat liberally with bread crumbs.

In a bowl, mix the egg with the milk and stir well to break up the egg. Add the egg-milk mixture to the potatoes, along with 2 tablespoons of the butter, the salt, and the grated Parmesan cheese, and mix well, mashing the potatoes to a smooth consistency.

Spread half of the potato mixture into the prepared pan, using a wooden spoon to even it out.

Scatter the mozzarella and the mortadella evenly on top of the potatoes. Cover with the rest of the potato mixture. Dot with the remaining 2 tablespoons of butter and sprinkle on the bread crumbs.

Place in the preheated oven, on the top rack, and bake until heated through and browned, 25 to 30 minutes.

eating with an italian mama of your own

Do you want to have an Italian mama cook for you? Or maybe teach you how to cook? You can actually do this without finding your own Italian wife or husband. Home Food is an association of home cooks throughout Italy who welcomes guests into their homes for meals. These are not "pop-up" restaurants, or anything "underground," just women who are keeping alive local traditions in their homes. It's a fantastic way to sample regional home cooking. The home cooks are called *le Cesarine,* and are located throughout Italy. The nonprofit organization is not about making money, but about sharing a way of life. Each home cook decides on his or her menu, then posts their availability on the website. There are now so many Cesarine that it's pretty easy to coordinate a meal in one of their homes with your travel plans. If you don't see an appropriate date, just send them a note, and they'll try to arrange a unique experience for you, which can also include a cooking lesson.

I first discovered Home Food while researching *Gourmet's Diary of a Foodie.* We featured Paola, a transplanted Sardinian woman now living in Rome. Her meal mixed her Sardinian roots with foods from her newfound home. Paola's menu included bucatini all'amatriciana, stewed rabbit, and mixed wild greens. The wine was from Sardinia, the table was set with family heirlooms, and the conversation lively with two other couples—one from Canada and the other from Australia—all happy to come together in a true Roman home.

sunday lunch
the best meal of the week

There were a lot of things in Italy that it took me a long time to get used to: Shops closing in the middle of the day. Unannounced strikes. Late trains. But one thing I took to immediately was the idea of a big Sunday lunch.

I grew up in a family where dinner was the only serious meal of the day and breakfast was a nonevent. Growing up in St. Louis, I guess we had cereal like most other kids at that time, and I do in fact have strong memories of preferring the pink to the green marsh-mallows in Lucky Charms. But even that weak attempt at a healthy breakfast flew out the window when we moved to Italy. I have strong memories of fending for myself on the way to catch the school bus by picking up a piece of pizza bianca at the bakery in the Jewish Ghetto. If I was extra hungry I would stop at the pizza al taglio place down the street and get a huge slice of what I called "salad pizza": pizza bianca topped with artichokes, arugula, and hard-boiled eggs.

But once my family hit the road, for long trips across Europe, all bets were off. Breakfast would consist of Tic Tacs from my mother's purse, passed to us at the crack of dawn from the front seat. To this day my sister Robin gags at the mere sound of those bright green mints clicking in their little plastic box.

Lunch in my family was similarly frowned upon and never really a sit-down planned affair. In fact, my mother still "picks" at lunch, poking around Tupperware containers straight from the refrigerator. She is never happier than while standing up at the counter, digging into last night's leftover salad, soggy and wilted from its overnight soak.

My father instead considers a big lunch an enormous waste of calories and/or a sign of weakness. For him dinner is the main meal and he would rather go hungry the entire day, packing in a day's worth of eating in one meal.

Luckily, at the international school that my sisters and I attended during our time in Italy lunch was—true to Italian tradition—the big meal of the day. Served cafeteria-style (that part was pure American), the food itself was 100 percent Roman. There was always a first course, pasta; and a second course, meat. I am pretty sure this is where my sister Jodi started her lifelong love affair with gnocchi. And it is certainly where I discovered that some people actually did sit down to a big lunch.

When I moved back to Italy, and to Florence, in 1988, as an adult to work on my dissertation, I had to face my family's ingrained lunch issues. Particularly, I had to decide what camp I was in. Was lunch a meal that was best eaten on the run, a quick panino wolfed down between bouts

of deciphering Latin documents? Or was it a time to sit down, rest, and refuel in order to face the rest of the day?

While most of my time in Florence was spent poring through sixteenth-century ledgers, documenting the shopping habits of the Medicis, with barely any time to think about lunch one way or the other, I was faced with endlessly long Sundays when the libraries and archives were closed. I am pretty sure it was my friend Marietta who suggested we fill our time off with a long and leisurely lunch. While during the week I made do with panini from the bar around the corner from the archive, on Sundays Marietta and I headed to our local trattoria for a full three-course meal with at least one liter of the house wine to wash it down. A walk and a nap followed, and I can't think of a more perfect formula for a Sunday afternoon in Italy.

While I thoroughly enjoyed my Sundays in Florence, I think I only learned to appreciate the true meaning of Sunday lunch once I was living in Rome and raising my own family. During the week, our main meal of the day was dinner. Weektime lunches, instead, tended to be quick things—leftovers, bread and cheese, or a panino from the bar. Not quite my mother's "picking" nor my father's "deprivation," but not a regular Italian lunch either.

Come Sunday, though, I cooked bigtime. I very much took to the idea of being an Italian mama. If during the week I would make something light for dinner, Sunday mornings would see me at the stove with a big pot of sauce boiling away, a pork roast in the oven, or some other delicious, long-cooking dish that would fill the house with the smell of "Sunday." I finally understood my mother-in-law's perennial question to me almost every day: *"Che cosa cucini stamattina?"* ("What are you cooking this morning?") Because she could never quite get her head around the fact that I didn't spend my mornings as she had done for most of her life, cooking for her husband and sons, who would come home from work and school for lunch.

And while *what* I was cooking certainly matters (and is always a subject of family debate), it is more the ritual of the day itself that matters the most.

italian brunch

I can't write about Sunday lunch in Rome without saying something about the new trend of Sunday brunch. When I first started to see restaurants in Rome advertising Sunday brunch, I thought, "Finally!" I have to admit that even though I am beyond assimilated here in Italy, I still have random and totally unpredictable expat cravings. Reese's Peanut Butter Cups rank high, as do things like cheddar cheese and tacos. So when I first read the word *brunch,* images of pancakes, bacon and eggs, and bagels naturally started floating through my head.

I should have known by the timing of the first brunch we went to that something was off. As the restaurant was not open until 12:30, I thought that it was a late start to breakfast. As we sat down, the waiter came by to take our drinks order and explain that the buffet would be set up any minute. As I saw waiters tending to chafing dishes, I still had hopes for eggs and could almost convince myself that I smelled sausage.

But when we finally picked up our plates and joined the line, I was greeted with platters of prosciutto and melon, mozzarella, and bresaola. Those chafing dishes? Full of lasagna and eggplant parmigiana. The only things vaguely brunchlike were tiny squares of red pepper frittata that were clearly meant as appetizers.

I'm not really sure who made this decision, but the "b" in *brunch,* in Rome, officially stands for "buffet," not "breakfast." Things would be much clearer if they just decided to call it "bunch" or "luffet" because it really just is a fixed-price lunch buffet, meant to be a more relaxed approach to Sunday lunch. I've never become a big fan, but I think this has more to do with my own personal antibuffet views than any judgment on the quality of the food. Because some of the "brunches" around Rome are quite good, and are hugely popular—even if there are no pancakes in sight.

when in rome . . . sunday lunch

- *Ordering:* This is your chance to order big. If you've been avoiding ordering more than one course during the week, this is the time to do the full *antipasto/primo/secondo* thing.

- *Timing:* With all that food, take your time. Sunday lunch is a long affair. At least two hours, usually much more, especially if you're invited to someone's house.

- *Passeggiata:* Walk it off with a long stroll afterward. This is what the Sunday *passeggiata* was invented for.

sunday lunch in rome

While there are lots of new restaurants that have opened in Rome over the last ten years, when it comes to Sunday lunch I am very old-school. I want a place that hasn't changed in decades. Because many families go out for lunch on Sunday, places do fill up ahead of time, so make sure you call to reserve at least a couple of days before.

Perilli
Via Marmorata 39, 39-06-574-2415

➤ This is our all-time favorite place for Sunday lunch. Evidently it's also everyone else's since it's near to impossible to get a Sunday lunch reservation here unless you call a few days ahead of time. But it's worth the effort. Founded in 1911, the old-fashioned place still has a distinct Roman trattoria feel to it. Located in Testaccio, where the old slaughterhouse was, it serves many dishes that feature those odd cuts of meat known as the quinto quarto, or the "fifth quarter" (i.e., offal). I think Perilli has the best carbonara in town, full of huge chunks of chewy guanciale. Sophie swears by the amatriciana (but then again, Sophie would probably order amatriciana even if she was in China). Either way, you can't go wrong. Unbutton your pants, and have a second course as well. I waffle among the *maialino* (roast suckling pig), the coratella (lamb innards), and the osso buco. See chapter 18 for more about Perilli.

Piperno
Monte de Cenci 9, 39-06-6880-6629

➤ I've been going here since I was twelve, and have a soft spot for this place. When my father can be convinced to have lunch, this is where we go. Not just because it's the closest restaurant to his house and he doesn't have to walk but also because it has excellent food. On a summer afternoon, you can't beat this jewel-size piazza for pretty, and in winter the green cloth–covered walls make the old-fashioned dining room extra cozy. What to get? Carciofi alla giudea (deep-fried artichokes), which is one of their specialties, or really anything fried, including zucchini and zucchini flowers. Save room for their *pala di nono* (grandfather's balls): deep-fried, chocolate-speckled balls of ricotta. I've never had them anywhere else (and not quite sure I need to).

La Campana

Vicolo della Campana 18, 39-06-687-5273

➤ La Campana is supposed to be Rome's oldest restaurant, with documents dating back to 1518. Well . . . whatever. It certainly is a Roman classic, with the same family running things just as they always have for generations. If you want to pick at least one old-fashioned traditional restaurant in Rome, this would be a good choice. The interiors are Roman comfortable and sober. Professional waiters in white jackets wait on tables draped in starched linen. The dishes are equally classic. This is where you go to have seasonal treats like vignarola, a soup made of spring artichokes, peas, and fava beans. I often choose fish, especially if it's Friday, and recently had an excellent grilled sole. But on Sunday, I tend to go the meat route. I love their veal sautéed in Marsala wine; it is as comforting as it sounds. Desserts are homemade, like their pear cake and *monte bianco* when chestnuts are in season.

places to have sunday brunch in rome

I overcome my "brunchaphobia" in Rome for a few places:

Lanificio

Via di Pietralata 159/159a, 39-06-4178-0081

➤ In an odd part of town, out the Nomentana road, Lanificio is located in an old wool factory along the banks of the Aniene River. The space itself is beyond perfect. Rough concrete floors, light flooding in, and the entire place furnished in mismatched chairs, tables, and couches. Kind of like a flea market, which I guess it is, because everything is for sale. The food is pretty good too, set up on two long wooden tables.

Open Colonna

Via Milano 9a, 39-06-4782-2641

➤ Open Colonna is overseen by one of Italy's most famous chefs, Antonello Colonna. Both his upscale, fancy restaurant and the more casual Open Colonna are located atop the Palazzo delle Esposizioni, encased in a steel and glass structure that sits on the roof of the museum. Their brunch buffet on the weekends is one of the most popular in town.

recipes for a sunday lunch

In our house it's always pasta.

bucatini all'amatriciana

Serves 4 to 5

3 thick slices of guanciale, chopped
into small cubes (you can substitute
pancetta or unsmoked bacon)

2 tablespoons extra-virgin olive oil, as needed

1 small onion, chopped

Hot red pepper flakes (optional)

One 28-ounce (794-gram) can peeled, whole San Marzano tomatoes with their juices

1 pound (500 grams) bucatini

½ cup grated Pecorino Romano cheese, or more as needed

Place the guanciale in a large sauté pan over medium heat and let it cook and sizzle until just starting to brown; it should give up quite a bit of fat. Turn off heat and, using a slotted spoon, scoop the guanciale bits up and set aside.

If there isn't a lot of rendered fat left in the pan, add a bit of olive oil. (You may not need to. There should be at least 3 to 4 tablespoons of fat.) Turn the heat back on, add the onion, and cook over low heat until quite soft, but not browned. At this point you can add a bit of red pepper flakes if you like to give it some kick.

Add the tomatoes and their juices to the pan, along with reserved guanciale. Let the sauce bubble away slowly for at least a half hour. It should reduce quite a bit, and thicken. If you think it's getting too thick, add a bit of water.

Bring a large pot of salted water to a boil. Add the bucatini and cook until al dente.

Drain the pasta, reserving a cup of the water, and transfer it to the pan with the sauce. Stir to combine, and cook briefly over gentle heat, just to meld the flavors. Remove from the heat, and stir in the cheese. If the sauce seems too thick, add a bit of reserved pasta water.

Serve with extra cheese on the side at the table.

pasta al forno

Serves 6

2 to 3 small eggplants (about 1 pound or ½ kilo total)

2 tablespoons extra-virgin olive oil, plus more for frying eggplant, oiling pan, and drizzling

2 garlic cloves, chopped

Hot red pepper flakes

4 cups (1 liter) tomato puree

Salt

1 pound (500 grams) pasta (I like shells, but you can use rigatoni, too)

1½ cups cubed smoked scamorza cheese

About 12 fresh basil leaves, torn

1 cup grated Parmesan cheese

Chop the eggplants into ½-inch cubes. In a high-sided pot, fry the eggplant cubes in about 2 inches of hot olive oil until golden and soft. Make sure not to overcrowd the pot. You may have to do this in a few batches. Remove the eggplant with a slotted spoon and transfer to paper towels to drain.

Heat the 2 tablespoons of olive oil in

a saucepan. Add the garlic and cook, stirring, for 1 minute. Stir in the red pepper flakes to taste. Add the tomato puree and salt to taste. Cook over low heat until it starts to thicken, about 15 minutes. Add torn basil leaves and stir. Taste and adjust with more salt if needed.

Cook the pasta in salted water until al dente. Drain and toss with some olive oil so it doesn't stick together.

Preheat the oven to 400°F (200°C). Rub an 8-by-12-inch casserole dish with olive oil.

In a large bowl, mix the pasta with the tomato sauce. Add the fried eggplant and gently stir to combine. Stir in 1 cup of the cubed scamorza. Pour the pasta into the prepared casserole dish. Top with the remaining ½ cup of cubed scamorza and the grated Parmesan and drizzle with olive oil.

Place in the preheated oven and bake until bubbly and browned on top, about 20 minutes.

Let sit for about 5 minutes before serving.

rome's perfect restaurant (at least for me)

When I first started thinking of this book, I was joking around that I should just title it *Favorite Restaurants in Rome* and be done with it. Because, let me tell you, if you are an expat living in Rome that is the question you get at least five times a week. "My dentist's aunt is coming to Rome. Can you recommend a great pizzeria?" "My ex-brother-in-law's girlfriend's niece will be spending her junior year abroad, can you list your ten favorite places to eat dinner that don't cost too much?" "Hi, you don't know me, but I went to high school with your sister. I'm in Rome right now. Could you tell me where to have lunch? Now?"

I'm not really exaggerating. And the thing is, I'm not the only one who gets these requests. All of my friends who live here in Rome are bombarded daily by friends of friends of friends who would like "the list." But, since I'm the food writer in our group, my friends always decide to field their queries to me. Thank you very much.

In the beginning, back at the dawn of time, I had a list that I would keep up to date. I'd either mail (remember stamps?) or fax (yes, really) this ever-changing list far and wide. Eventually the list got so passed around that it would make its way back to me in a culinary version of Six Degrees of Meal Planning. I would receive an e-mail from a total stranger, sending me "their" list of restaurants to comment on. "A friend of mine knows a chef who gave me his list of favorite places. Can you tell me if you agree with him?" "Well, yes, actually I can, since this is the list I gave to the chef last year before his trip to Rome."

As we moved into the digital age I think one of the very first things I threw up on the Web was something called Elizabeth's Restaurants. At least, now, I could easily direct everyone to a simple website without the need for stamps and/or fax paper.

And then blogs happened and, before I knew it, my idea of posting a simple list of restaurants transformed itself into a forum where I could talk about so much more. This finally led to my app, *Eat Rome*. This, I thought, would finally eliminate the need of anyone to ask me questions about Roman restaurants ever again. It was all there, constantly updated, easily downloaded, and, frankly, dirt cheap. Now I (and all my fellow expats in Rome) could respond with a very short e-mail: Buy the app.

And most people do. But you want to know something? Even though I spent an awful lot of time pulling together my list of favorites in Rome? The e-mails still continue to arrive from people asking me to narrow the list down. What are your favorite five restaurants? What's your favorite place to have pizza? Where should we go for a predinner glass of wine?

And, since *Eat Rome* lists more than 80

restaurants, I still continue to get asked the following question on an almost daily basis: What is your very, very favorite place to eat?

How am I supposed to answer that? There are so many variables. It depends on the weather and the season. It depends on how I'm feeling, and how much money I want to spend. Do I feel like getting dressed up? Do I want to take a taxi or drive? Or should I just stay in my own neighborhood? This is not a straightforward question, and there is really no simple answer. Sorry.

That said, a couple of years ago I reconsidered all of this. There had just been a major earthquake in central Italy. The online world was all atwitter with predictions of an impending rapture or something. So I finally got to thinking: What would my very last meal in Rome be if I had to choose? My very last meal if I would never be in Rome again? Before I got raptured up to heaven or sucked down when the Earth split open? No one had ever asked me that before.

And, if you put it that way, the answer is easy: Perilli, Via Marmorata 39.

This old-fashioned Testaccio trattoria has been going strong since 1911. And even if they recently spruced up the place, the important things remain the same. Certainly the food and—I suspect—even some of the waiters haven't changed in decades. I guess some people are a bit put off by the fact that it feels like an insiders-only Roman place to go. And in fact, you'll find few tourists there (especially at Sunday lunch). It always has been, and remains, a place frequented by regulars, of which I am definitely one.

While I love the waiters (Valerio is my favorite), and the slightly frumpy overlit, mural-covered dining room, of course what keeps me coming back is the food. My favorite dish: hands down the carbonara. This is (and you heard it here) the best carbonara in Rome. Al dente rigatoni bathed in a wet gooey coating of egg and cheese, studded with huge chewy chunks of guanciale. I could eat it three times a day, every day.

As I've already explained, my daughter Sophie would kill for a plate of their bucatini all'amatriciana. Since we usually head here for Sunday lunch, we manage to make it through at least two courses. Their roast pork and roast lamb are both covered in crispy, salty skin, moist and tender on the inside and served with what may be the best roast potatoes in town. In spring I sometimes skip the meat, and get a heaping portion of vignarola (a springtime stew of artichokes, peas, and fava beans). (OK, I never skip the meat, but get both meat and vignarola.) Since this is Testaccio, there is offal galore: *rigatoni con la pajata* (rigatoni with lamb's intestines) and coratella (lamb innards) are favorites. I also love the osso buco, smothered in fresh peas. But no matter how much we manage to eat, Emma, who has the sweet tooth in the family, always saves room for the rich and creamy old-fashioned zabaione.

When you go (notice I didn't say "if"), and more than one person at the table orders carbonara, make sure *you* get the serving bowl. After serving out portions of pasta to the table, one lucky diner gets to eat his or her pasta straight out of the serving bowl. This means extra cheesy, eggy gooeyness and all those stray pieces of guanciale (cured pork jowl) that sink to the bottom.

But there are other things that help me define "favorite restaurant." I have to admit that one of them is convenience. There is a reason we all have our "neighborhood" place. In theory, I love trying out new restaurants, and of course I do this a lot not only for my work but also for my pleasure. I say "in theory" because, of course, I'm like everyone else I know. Those reservations you made weeks ago, to go to the newest, hottest restaurant across town, seemed like a good idea at the time. But come 7:30 p.m., after a full day of work, all you really want to do is walk around the corner to your neighborhood trattoria. Not only are you known and loved (cue the theme from *Cheers*), but you also know and love what will be on your plate. Am I right?

And then there is the whole question of defining "favorite." In my book, favorite doesn't necessarily mean someplace I eat at every week. Some of my favorite places in Rome are restaurants that I sometime make it to only once a year. But—and this is a big but—they are restaurants I've been going to once a year for about thirty

years now. These are the classics, the old-fashioned Roman restaurants I've been going to since I was twelve years old.

This is the type of restaurant that is often ignored by foodies and guidebooks: the old-fashioned, more formal spots simply called ristoranti. Not trattoria, osteria, or any other *-ria,* but the kind of place that has existed for decades. When I first moved to Rome, in the early '70s, these were the places we would go as a special treat. Forty years later, I am still dining at these institutions, and many of the same waiters are still shuffling about in white jackets, transporting plates of gnocchi and deep-fried salt cod. These are the old-school haunts where you are more likely to be seated next to an Italian senator or film director than someone you know from San Francisco.

my favorite classics in rome

Ristorante Nino

Via Borgognona 11, 39-06-679-5676

➢ Nino, near the Spanish Steps, doesn't get much attention—which is strange, since the food has been consistently excellent since I began dining here, in 1972. The restaurant, opened in 1934, bills itself as Tuscan, and it certainly serves a superb *zuppa di fagioli* (bean soup). But what I really love about Nino are the old-style dishes that seem like holdovers from a 1960s Italian country club menu, including *sformato di spinaci* (a cup-size spinach soufflé served with chicken liver or tomato sauce) and the best steak tartare in town.

Piperno

Monte de' Cenci 9, 39-06-688-06629

➢ Open since 1860, Piperno is my father's favorite restaurant in Rome. We dined here every Sunday when we lived above this justifiably well-known spot. Decades later, my family still gathers here to celebrate birthdays and anniversaries. If it's summer, make sure you ask for a table outside, in what is one of the smallest, and most beautiful, of the city's piazzas. This is Rome's ancient Jewish Ghetto, and the menu pays tribute to the neighborhood's heritage.

Pompiere

Via Santa Maria dei Calderari 38, 39-06-686-8377

➢ Located not far from Piperno, Pompiere is another family favorite. It is somewhat hidden up a flight of stairs—the prime reason few know about it. This gem is separated into four huge rooms, some of which have frescoed ceilings, making it perfect for large groups. Grilled veal chops and fried zucchini flowers are the house specialties, and some charmingly outdated dishes, such as the *linguine al limone* (linguine with lemon and cream), are hard to find anywhere else.

Al Moro

Vicolo delle Bollette 13, 39-06-678-3495

➤ This is the one old-school institution that most people know. Located a coin's throw from the Trevi Fountain, Al Moro is a likely spot for bumping into politicians or captains of industry taking very long lunches. What are they lounging over? Vignarola (a stew of fava beans, peas, and artichokes), osso buco, and a pasta all'arrabbiata. The traditional menu changes to reflect the seasons, but the slightly grumpy waiters won't tell you anything about the dishes unless you ask. Do. It's worth it.

La Campana

Vicolo della Campana 18, 39-06-687-5237

➤ La Campana bills itself as the oldest restaurant in Rome (circa the seventeenth century), and maybe it is. All I know is that today it's always full of Italian families with well-dressed children. The biggest draw is the excellent food, especially the antipasti, which is deliciously displayed inside the front door. (All restaurants used to do this, but few still do.) I always order *saltimbocca,* a classic dish of sautéed veal with prosciutto and sage. But no matter what I get, I always save room for the monte bianco, a fluffy mound of chestnut purée, whipped cream, and meringue.

recipes

There are certain dishes that I only order at these old-fashioned Roman restaurants.

osso buco

Serves 4

Osso buco, braised veal shank, is not really a Roman recipe. It is more commonly found in the north of Italy, especially around Milan, where it's served with *risotto alla milanese* (a saffron-scented risotto). In other words, like much of northern Italian cooking it is considered to be more sophisticated than the rough-and-tumble world of rustic Roman cooking, which is why you often find it on the menus of old-fashioned Roman restaurants. It is their attempt at fancy, although of course it's anything but. A huge slice of veal shank is stewed until it almost falls apart. My favorite rendition of this dish is at Perilli. Like the Milanese version, it is done *in bianco,* stewed simply in a sauce of white wine and broth. When I make it at home, which I rarely do, I usually use a mixture of carrot, celery, and onion.

Four 1-inch-thick slices osso buco
Salt
Freshly ground black pepper
1 large onion

1 large carrot

1 large leek

1 large fennel bulb

¼ cup (330 milliliters) extra-virgin olive oil

2 tablespoons unsalted butter

All-purpose flour, for dredging

1 cup (230 milliliters) dry white wine

Zest from 1 untreated lemon

1 small bunch flat-leaf parsley

Season the osso buco with salt and pepper and let sit for about 20 minutes.

In the meantime, chop the vegetables. I usually just put everything into the food processor. I like chopped, but pretty fine, so that makes the job go much more quickly.

Heat the olive oil and butter in a pan large enough to hold all the meat and the vegetables.

Dredge the osso buco in flour and add to the pan, and brown well over high heat, on both sides. By brown well, I mean really brown well. Do not skimp on this part. Those rich, dark brown bits of caramelized meat are what will give the rest of the dish its rich, deep taste. Remove the osso buco and place aside on a plate.

Add all the vegetables to the pan. Using a wooden spoon, scrape up the browned bits of meat and flour from the bottom. Let the vegetables cook, until softened, about 10 minutes. Season with salt.

Add the meat and any juices back to the pan, pushing aside the vegetables to make room.

Add the wine and simmer for about 4 minutes. Cover the pan and let cook for about 15 minutes, then check to see if it's too dry. If so, add about a cup of water, cover again, and cook very slowly for about an hour.

Chop the lemon zest and parsley finely, then add them to the osso buco at the last minute. You don't have to stir it in (it will be hard to do so), but make sure you've managed to get some *gremolata* on each piece.

Serve each guest a piece of osso buco with the sauce. Of course the best way to enjoy the sauce is along with a big mound of buttery mashed potatoes.

saltimbocca

Serves 4

A lot of people have a hard time with the word *saltimbocca.* And, in fact, it does sound slightly odd, until you realize that it is Roman dialect for *saltare in bocca,* or "jump in your mouth." This dish, made from thin slices of veal paired with prosciutto and sage, is so good, the thinking goes, that it literally jumps up into your mouth. These days the dish has become famous and appears on Italian restaurant menus all over the

(continued)

world—except, of course, in Rome. At some point it just fell off the radar of most restaurants as just too old-fashioned. But there are a still a few places, like Pompiere and La Campana, where I almost never pass it up.

1 pound (500 grams) thin veal scallops

Salt

Freshly ground black pepper

12 fresh sage leaves

12 thin slices thinly sliced prosciutto crudo di Parma

1 tablespoon unsalted butter

1 tablespoon extra-virgin olive oil

¾ cup (80 milliliters) dry white wine

Using a meat mallet or a rolling pin, flatten each of the scallops as thinly as possible. Season with salt and pepper.

Place a sage leaf atop each scallop, top with a slice of prosciutto, and attach to the scallop with one or two toothpicks.

Heat a large frying pan over high heat and add the butter and oil. When the butter has stopped foaming, add as many scallops as possible, veal side down. Cook for 2 minutes and then flip over and let cook for another minute. They should be browned and be thoroughly cooked. Set aside in a warm dish and repeat to cook the rest of the meat. Add the wine, scraping up the browned bits on the bottom of the pan, and return the meat to the pan and coat with the sauce.

Place the veal on a warm platter and top with the pan juices. Make sure to warn everyone about the toothpicks.

Note: You can also roll the veal up into individual little bundles, which are easier to cook and handle. But not as pretty, I think.

recipes made with cream and butter

There is an entire class of recipes that popped up in the '50s in Italy. It was a time when the country was coming out of the privations of World War II and so cooks and chefs were ready to embrace not only a newfound abundance, but ingredients that almost screamed richness. Heavy cream and butter featured prominently. Though these traditionally had almost no place in central Italian cooking, chefs at more upscale restaurants began to develop and serve pastas that were slippery with a slick of these heavy ingredients. This is the period that gave birth to fettuccine Alfredo and tagliolini al limone. Both of these dishes remind me somehow of the food I grew up with at the country club in suburban St. Louis—rich and comforting, and always served by a waiter in a white jacket.

fettuccine alfredo

Serves 4

After this dish was invented and served at this classic Italian restaurant, the name Alfredo came to mean anything with a cream and cheese sauce on it. The original dish is purer: consisting of fettuccine, butter, and grated cheese. It is not very Roman at all, except that it is.

1 pound (500 grams) fresh fettuccine
6 tablespoons (¾ stick/80 grams) unsalted butter, at room temperature
¾ cup finely grated Parmesan cheese

Bring a large pot of salted water to a boil. Place a large serving platter in the oven to warm.

Drop the pasta into the boiling water. When the pasta is cooked al dente, take the warmed serving platter out of the oven (careful not to burn your hands) and place the butter, in small pieces, on the dish. Lift out the pasta from the boiling water using tongs, letting some of the water cling to the noodles, and place it atop the butter on the platter. Using two forks, begin to toss the pasta, adding the cheese, handful by handful. A nice creamy sauce should start to form. If it seems too dry, you can add a few tablespoons of the pasta cooking water. Serve immediately.

tagliolini al limone

Serves 4

This is what I always order at Pompiere, the classic Roman restaurant located at the edge of the Jewish Ghetto on the second floor of Palazzo Cenci.

6 tablespoons (¾ stick/80 grams) unsalted butter
Finely grated zest of 2 large untreated lemons
1 pound (500 grams) fresh tagliolini (or other thinly cut fresh egg pasta)
½ cup (120 milliliters) heavy cream, at room temperature
½ cup finely chopped fresh flat-leaf parsley

Melt the butter in a sauté pan large enough to hold the cooked pasta. Add the lemon zest and heat for 1 minute. Remove from the heat.

Bring a large pot of salted water to a boil. Add the pasta and cook just until it is almost done; the pasta will continue to cook as you dress it.

Place the pan with the butter back over the heat and, using tongs, lift the pasta out of the water and into the pan with the butter. Stir to combine and gradually add the heavy cream, letting it thicken slightly. If it gets too thick, use a bit of pasta cooking water to thin it out. Serve in heated bowls, topped with parsley.

how to eat gelato like a roman

One of the most dangerous things you can do in Rome is head out for a gelato without a plan. OK, it's maybe not the most dangerous thing (that would be crossing the street as a pedestrian), but if you're not careful about where you buy your cone you may be in for a very horrible experience.

You probably think I'm exaggerating, but I'm not. When my daughters, Sophie and Emma, were eight and five, we unwittingly stopped by a gelateria that we didn't know on our way back from their music lesson. Emma was always easy to please, if messy, since she always chose chocolate. Sophie, who usually ordered only strawberry and lemon, decided to go wild and order banana. While my little drama queen was known to blow things out of proportion (especially when it came to food), her first gagging on, then spitting out the mouthful of bright yellow gelato was fully justified. I tasted it, completely prepared to berate her for making such a fuss, but I too had to spit it out into a napkin. It was that gross.

If you're like a lot of other people, you are probably thinking Italy + Gelato = Good. How could a country that invented gelato let things go so wrong? It wasn't always so. Gelato in Italy, like many traditional favorites, has had its ups and downs over the last fifty years or so.

And if one of the first things you think of eating when you are in Italy is gelato, there is a good reason for that. Gelato, or ice cream, was pretty much invented here.

Frozen desserts, the ancestor of today's gelato, actually go back further than the Italian Renaissance. Ancient Romans, Egyptians, and Arabs crafted syrup-soaked, cooling sweets with snow brought down from mountaintops and stored in belowground cold rooms—more or less a type of literal snow cone without the cone.

Gelato as we know it today—the creamy and soft sweetened milk-and/or-fruit-based dessert—was invented in Florence during the Renaissance. In sixteenth-century Florence artists were jacks-of-all-trades, expected not only to paint, sculpt, and design buildings, but also to be on call for their clients should they need an extra-special event. Leonardo was known for his extraordinary fireworks.

One of the earliest and best-known party planners was Bernardo Buontalenti. Famous for his fantastical garden grottoes as well as more permanent architectural structures like palaces and churches, he was also master of the ephemeral. Huge entry gates and colorful backdrops were constructed of board and plaster to impress for a day and then be taken away, and terrifically elaborate firework displays were planned for marriages, pageants, and coronations.

Could this focus on the fleeting element of visual spectacle have inspired him to create a dish that could melt before your eyes if not gobbled up quickly? I like to think so, since it was Buontalenti who dished up the first serving of gelato to Catherine de' Medici in 1565. His unique refrigerating techniques allowed him to turn sugar and milk into a frozen novelty that seduced everyone at the party. It was another Italian, Francesco Procopio dei Coltelli, who popularized the dessert, by opening his café, Procope, in Paris, where he dished up gelato for one and all, not just princesses at their parties.

In Italy, gelato remained, for centuries, a rare and much-appreciated treat. Rare because not only did you have to get your hands on expensive ingredients like milk, sugar, and eggs to create it, but also you needed some form of refrigeration, which, before the invention of electricity, was not the flick of a switch it is today. Carrying down natural ice from a mountaintop to churn your dessert was not an everyday event.

Things started to change in a big way in Italy after World War II. Not only did refrigeration become more common, access to primary ingredients after wartime shortages meant more and more commercial establishments began to sell gelato.

In Rome, many of the first places to become *gelaterie*—places that sold gelato—were *latterie*, or stores that sold milk. Obviously they had access to the main ingredient and, with the addition of seasonal fruit, nuts, chocolate, and other natural flavors, began to make gelato a more affordable and regular snack.

As with all food-related things over the

last fifty years, progress has had an unfortunate effect on gelato in Italy. While there are still some old-fashioned gelaterie making gelato with natural ingredients such as real fruit and nuts, the majority of places you run into in the more heavily "touristed" areas of town churn their ice cream from premade mixes or buy industrially premade gelato.

Thankfully, in the last few years, there has been a renaissance of artisanal gelaterie. A return to all natural ingredients and attention to quality means that it's not as hard as it was about twelve years ago to get a good scoop. One of the pioneers of this mini gelato revolution in Rome is Claudio Torcè. His insistence on going back to basics and sourcing the best ingredients means that there are a growing number of places in Rome where you can find gelato made not just from fresh pistachios, but from the best pistachios in the world, grown only in the small Sicilian town of Bronte. The eggs are not just any organic eggs, but eggs lovingly raised by Paolo Parisi in Tuscany, and the chocolate, single varietals from Venezuela.

How can you tell a good gelateria from a bad one? Here are a few clues:

- *Color:* Is the gelato brighter than any fruit known in nature? Chances are, those neon green and shocking pink tones come from added food coloring. While some fruits, like strawberries, are naturally bright, others, like

bananas and pistachios, should always be a rather unappetizing shade of khaki.

- *Shape:* Is the gelato displayed in great fluffy mounds that defy gravity? If so, run the other way. Gelato does not attain this shape naturally, and great waves of cream and color usually betray the addition of gelatin, stabilizers, and other ingredients that have no place in traditional gelato.

- *Seasonality:* Although some flavors like chocolate and pistachio are available year-round, others, like strawberry and chestnut, should only make their appearance while in season. If you're seeing raspberry in January and persimmon in August, then it's likely either the fruit was frozen (if you're lucky) or the entire thing is made from a premade or artificial mix.

when in rome . . . gelato rules

Like everything else in Italy involving food, there are certain ways to eat gelato.

- *When to eat gelato:* In general, Italians don't eat between meals. But gelato falls into the category of *merenda,* or late-afternoon snack. Heading out for a gelato anytime from 4:00 to 7:00 p.m. is pretty standard. It took me quite a long time to get into this idea of having a predinner cone, but somehow that is still considered snacktime, since dinner doesn't come on until a couple of hours later.

- *How to eat gelato:* Choose your flavor. The gelato will be displayed in refrigerated cases. The better gelato places store their gelato in stainless steel bins with lids to limit the exposure to air, which affects the flavor and freshness. In this case have a look at the printed flavors, and be ready. By the way, Italians do not ask for tastes of different flavors before deciding which one to commit to—ever!

- *Choose your size:* The sizes and prices are often displayed behind or on the counter. There will usually be three sizes of little paper cups and one size cone, which you can have topped with one to three flavors. Generally, even in the smallest cups you are allowed to have two flavors. And that large size? If you're thinking that the large size doesn't look that large compared to even the smallest of the sizes you're used to in America, you're right. Most Italians will opt for the smallest size, which is just a quarter to a third of a cup. Those big sizes? *Troppo!* And usually only ordered by foreigners who don't know any better.

- *Panna?* Once you've decided on your size and your flavor, the person serving you will ask you a one-word question: *"Panna?"* ("Whipped cream?") Almost all Italians expect and enjoy a big dollop of whipped cream on their cone or cup. When it's good, it's great. It's almost always unsweetened, and some of the older gelaterie still have their original whipped cream machines, which somehow whip at a lower speed, which results in an even creamier texture.

- *Paying:* This is something that drives me insane in gelaterie. Although some of the bigger places insist that you pay ahead of time at the cash register and then bring your receipt to the person serving the gelato, most of the smaller ones have a different system. They hand you your filled cone, then tell you how much to pay. Which means that you are holding your cone with one hand, while you desperately try to dig into your purse or wallet with the other, to pay. All over Rome. All the time.

- *Walk and talk:* Whether in a cup or in a cone, gelato is street food, meant to be consumed while taking a leisurely passeggiata.

- *Gelato sitting down:* While many of the new breed of gelaterie are small places, with no tables or places to sit down, some of the older bars that also serve great gelato do have table service. But beware: When ordering a cone or cup directly from the counter, you are not

allowed to take it with you to a table and sit down. The tables are serviced by waiters, who will take your order and come back to you with a glass or metal cup filled with a larger portion of gelato. The service naturally comes with a price, but you also get a chance to sit down, and you will be served water as well.

where to eat gelato in rome

Claudio Torcè

Viale Aventino 59

➤ Among the half dozen top-notch artisan gelaterie in Rome these days, this one is at the top of the list. Over the years I've tried, I think, most of the flavors. My favorites? Don't be shocked, but I love both the celery and the habanero. I know they sound strange, but they weren't. *Brie con frutti di bosco* (Brie with berries) is creamy and just cheesy enough. Don't worry, they have normal flavors, too.

Fatamorgana

Piazza degli Zingari, 39-06-8639-1589

➤ Following in the footsteps of Claudio Torcè, Fatamorgana was one of the first artisanal gelaterie in Rome to start playing around with weird and wonderful ingredients. Kentucky is a heavenly mix of chocolate and tobacco. My favorite is Dukha, a Middle Eastern–inspired mélange of sesame seeds, hazelnuts, and coriander. And

then there are flavors like pear and Gorgonzola, which must be popular since it's always freshly made. But don't worry, they also do the classics, so you are sure to find whatever fruit is in season, whipped up into cool and creamy perfection. There are now several other locations in different parts of town.

Alberto Pica

Via della Seggiola 12, 39-06-688-06153

➤ I can still remember the taste of the melon ice cream I had here in 1972. I was twelve, and we were living across the street. After lunch I begged to be let out on my own to get a gelato. By the time I made it back upstairs, I had finished my small cup of *melone*. It was so good, I immediately left again, to get another cup. What I really loved was the way the pure, rich whipped cream became almost solid next to the cold gelato.

Even back in those days, I was surprised I had enough nerve to go there on my own. And it had nothing to do with crossing the street. Pica was, back then, and continues to be today, well known for its gruff owners. But if you can get past the Roman attitude, the ice cream is heavenly. They are best known for their rice-based gelati, which change according to whim and season. How does the rice stay so firm? A closely guarded secret! Domenico's favorite is the zabaione, made with egg yolks and Marsala wine. I love the *riso alla canella* (rice with cinnamon). And I will stand by my word that they make the very best pistachio gelato I've ever had in my life.

Gracchi

Via dei Gracchi 272, 39-06-321-6668

➢ Why does Prati, the neighborhood around the Vatican, have such a high concentration of great gelaterie? I guess it's because it's so densely residential, as well as having some great shopping districts; in other words, a lot of foot traffic.

Gelateria Gracchi is just a block away from the busy shopping street of Cola di Rienzo, and close enough to the Vatican for an easy stroll. This place, though, is worth a hike for its seasonal, carefully crafted gelati. I always think that a test of any ice cream place is their nut flavors, and Gelateria Gracchi comes out with flying colors. Both pistachio and hazelnut with meringue are creamy and full of big chunks of nuts. Their seasonal menu means you may not always find everything, but their autumn persimmon is out of this world, like biting into a big juicy piece of fruit. My hands-down favorite is roasted chestnut, available only a few short months of the year. (They just opened a new location on Via dell'Angeletto in the Monti neighborhood.)

Come il Latte

Via Silvio Spaventa 24–26, 39-06-429-03882

➢ While some of the new gelaterie are minimal in terms of the richness of their product, Come il Latte leans toward the creamy and rich side of things, but then goes several steps further. First of all, the flavors: very addictive and comfort-foody. I can't get enough of *caramello al sale* (salted caramel) and all of my Italian friends love the *mascarpone con biscotti Gentillini,* a sort of cream cheese flavor with an Italian brand of crunchy cookies scattered in. High-quality ingredients go without saying. And the crunchy cones and cookies that get stuck on top of each cup? They are first dipped or coated in chocolate that is running out of two faucets at the end of the counter. You have your choice of dark chocolate or white. Yes. For real.

other cold sweet treats in rome

Gelato is not the only thing to cool you off during a hot Roman summer. There are several other types of icy treats in which you can indulge.

Tazza d'Oro

Via degli Orfani 84, 39-06-678-9792

➢ Where to get the best coffee in Rome? Everyone has their favorite, but at the very top of the bunch there is Tazza d'Oro. If it's summer, run—don't walk—here to have the very best granita di caffè in town. This is served with freshly whipped cream, piled into the bottom of the cup as well as slathered on top. I like to ask for mine *solo sotto,* (only on the bottom), and then mush it all together with my spoon for a creamy coffee slushy treat.

Casa del Cremolato

(See the photograph below.)

Via Priscilla 18

➤ Although it's located out of the center of town, it's worth the effort to sample one of the best *cremolati* in Rome. If you've never had a cremolato, or even heard of one, it's a close relative of the granita. But while a granita is more about liquid, turning into icy delight, the cremolato is all about the fruit. Perfectly ripe fruit is combined with just enough sugar, frozen, and then mashed

up just enough to produce an intensely flavorful, fruity, and bone-chilling treat. There are big frozen chunks of fruit that almost hurt your teeth when you bite into them. It is the perfect antidote to a Roman summer heat wave. While you can certainly get a small paper cup to go, you should go for broke (it is a pain getting there) and take a seat at the cool '60s chairs and tables and order a heavy glass goblet filled to the brim with cremolato. Make sure you get whipped cream, which is still churned in their old-fashioned whipping machine, and one of the thickest and richest I've ever had.

Pascucci

Via di Torre Argentina 20

➤ I've been going to Pascucci for about forty years. Although they've recently renovated, there are still the same battery of industrial-strength blenders ready to whip the marinating fruit into icy-cold *frulatti,* or smoothies, which are served in old-fashioned soda fountain glasses. My favorite flavor is still Amalfi, a mix of citrus and strawberries; sweet, tart, and cold.

Grattachecca Sora Mirella

Lungotevere degli Anguillara (near the bridge to the Isola Tiberina)

➤ The *grattachecca* is a Roman tradition. The simplest and most rustic of summer treats, it is made from shaved ice that is topped with fruit syrup. There used to be stands all over the city that sold this treat,

but one of few remaining, and perhaps the most famous, is the one near the Tiber Island. A special metal tool is used to shave a huge block of ice, which, snowlike, is packed into a glass. A drizzle of the syrup of your choice—*amamrena,* or sour cherry, is my favorite—and that's that. Usually served with both a spoon and a straw, it can also be topped with fresh fruit.

gelato versus ice cream

What is the difference between gelato and ice cream? The answer: nothing. *Gelato* is simply the Italian word for the English *ice cream,* plain and simple. Are there differences between the Italian and the American product? Certainly! But as far as the word goes, your ice cream is my gelato. And vice versa.

One of the key differences in how both frozen desserts are made has to do with the machines used. In Italy the machines move more slowly and so incorporate much less air into the finished scoop. The result is a denser, thicker, and smoother-feeling frozen treat. Another factor is the higher butterfat content of American ice cream. So if you think that gelato in Italy tastes more intense, you're right. The additional air not only makes the taste in the States less intense, the higher butterfat content also coats your tongue, giving your taste buds less exposure to flavor.

{ chapter 20 }

learning to love roman pastries

have a confession to make. It took me a very long time to cozy up to eating pastries in Rome. When I lived in Paris, not a day would go by without a stop for an *éclair* or a *pain au chocolat*. But here in Rome, from the time I first lived here when I was twelve years old, displays of Roman pastries, or even the dessert part of menus, just never held my attention.

And, if you think about it, when you come to Rome, is your first thought to eat pastries? No, it's pizza or pasta, or some other form of savory carbohydrate. And when it comes to the sweet side of things, I'm sure you are more likely to Google "best gelato in Rome" than "best cornetti." Right?

To my mind, the pastries always looked to be trying too hard. Deep-fried *and* filled with pastry cream? Deep-fried *and* topped with powdered sugar? Or at the other end of the spectrum, hard dry cookies that could only begin to become attractive after being dunked in a cup of tea or glass of sweet wine, or both. I was never even tempted to try anything, so completely unappetizing did they seem.

But all that changed one rainy evening in Rome. I was walking through Trastevere with a friend who was living here for the year while working on his dissertation at the American Academy. Since he had been working on Baroque architecture for years (dissertations take a long time to write), he knew the alleyways of Rome pretty well. We were headed to the one theater in Rome that showed English language films at the time, the Pasquino. Known mostly for its retractable roof, which they would open during the summer, it was in all other respects a typical Italian cinema. And so, like all other cinemas in Italy there were no candy stands or popcorn for sale in the lobby, which meant my friend wanted to grab a snack before we went in.

Even though it was pouring down rain, and we were steps from the cinema, he force-marched us all across Piazza Santa Maria in Trastevere to a small pastry shop on an even smaller alley. I'd never been there before since the dusty windows never looked that promising. But he kept going on about getting a *bignè di San Giuseppe* because this was the last day he could get one. Bignè di San Giuseppe are made only in the days leading up to the festival of Saint Joseph, on March 19. Since it was March 18 this was going to be his very last chance to enjoy this treat.

And so we squeezed into the small shop and he gleefully ordered one of the deep-fried, cream-filled pastries I had been avoiding. It even had a maraschino cherry on the top, for god's sake. But his joy seemed so complete as he bit into the unwieldy bignè that I decided that maybe looks could be deceiving. Since he wasn't sharing any of his, I broke down and bought my own. And standing in the dim corner of this dusty pastry shop I finally got it. Although the pastry was fried, it was not greasy at all. And the cream that filled the center was

eggy, but not overly rich. And what seemed at first glance like a massive amount of sweetness to finish was gobbled up before I knew it.

From this point on I made it pretty much my new hobby to try all those pastries I had been avoiding for so long. Fried, cream-filled, ricotta-stuffed—it was all good. I was particularly fascinated by the many holiday treats I had been missing out on all those years. This is when the pastry shops go into high gear, preparing seasonal treats for Christmas, Easter, Carnevale, and varied saint's name days.

If Rome is not particularly known for its inventive sweets, Sicily certainly is. And, in fact, some of my favorite places to head for a pastry fix trace their origins back to Palermo.

Dagnino has got to be one of the strangest and most wonderful places in Rome. This Sicilian pastry shop is absolutely stuck in a time warp that takes you back to the late '60s. The setting is in a sort of underpass/mall that runs beneath a modern building from one street to another, a block from Piazza Repubblica. If you didn't know it was there, there's no way you would stumble upon it.

Why do I love it so much? First of all, the above-mentioned time-warp thing. The interiors have all the original decoration and furnishings: banquet seating, vintage murals, marble floors, and cloth-covered wooden tables.

I also love the colors. On a cold and windy

February afternoon there is something about the pastel tones of bright pink *gelato di campagna*, the moss green *cassata*, and glistening candied clementines that just makes me happy. I mean, who doesn't love looking at a bright and shiny row of marzipan tomatoes?

And the sound track to my reveries? A pianist (I kid you not) playing away on a shiny grand on Sunday afternoons.

But back to the pastries, which are what bring me here in the first place. While I usually go for one of the Sicilian specialties—a mini *cassata* or a cannoli—I'm just as likely to load up on whatever seasonal holiday sweets are on offer. If they have any sort of fried pastry stuffed with sweetened ricotta, just buy it, and ask questions later

Every neighborhood in Rome used to have at least one *pasticceria,* a place that would turn out cakes and pastries daily that would be bought up pretty much by people living in the neighborhood. When I first moved to Rome, ours was located right on the corner of Via Baccina and Via dei Serpenti. Pasticceria La Licata had been there since 1965 and was run by a couple from the neighborhood. This is where I ordered Sophie and Emma's first birthday cakes, and where we always stopped on the way back from the park for a sweet treat.

Sadly, once the mother died, the place closed. One daughter and son now run a very successful bar down the street. But the one son who was the pastry chef just couldn't make a go of it. Rising rents in the center of Rome meant that he had to look for a space farther out of town. And so, like many other pastry shops in the center of Rome, ours closed down. (The space is now a fast-food sushi shop.)

Thankfully there are still a few of these old-fashioned, traditional places left in some of Rome's more residential neighborhoods. And since they are so few and far between these days, the ones that are left are incredibly popular and have a huge following of fans.

Regoli is one of these. I can't seem to walk within a ten-block radius of this pastry shop without making a beeline for one of their incredibly rich, cream-stuffed, flaky delights.

Regoli is a family-run pastry shop that specializes in rich, cream-filled pastries that aren't always part of the Roman repertoire. The *bavarese* may be my downfall. I can't resist the two flaky layers of pastry that hold together a virtual slab of heavenly cream. The *fagottino alla ricotta* is a similar delight, switching in chocolate-studded ricotta for the cream.

If you are invited to a dinner, nothing can beat arriving with one of Regoli's famous cakes. Their ricotta tart is one of the best in Rome. Seasonal treats include the chestnut-filled monte bianco and the cream-filled individual tarts topped with wild strawberries.

One of my favorite bakeries in Rome is barely more than a counter in a dusty shop. Although its official name is Boccione, everyone just calls it Il Forno del Ghetto, or the "Jewish Bakery." I've been going there since I was twelve and lived down the street, and the burned sugary smell will lead you there from anywhere in the neighborhood.

The sisters who stand guard behind the counter, usually bickering among themselves, bake only about eight things, some changing with the Jewish holidays. Their specialty though—and what people wait in line for—is the *pizza ebraica,* a mix of dried fruit and nuts barely held together with a slightly sweet dough.

eating pastries in rome: old school

Pasticceria Siciliana Svizzera

Piazza Pio XI 10, 39-06-637-4947

➢ Sicily meets Switzerland in this neighborhood classic, up and behind the Vatican. Don't miss the mini cassate. If you happen by for breakfast, don't miss their Danese, their version of the iced Danish. And make sure you get one of their elaborate cream-filled cakes (that's where Switzerland meets Sicily) to go.

Dagnino

Via Emanuele Orlando 75, 39-06-481-8660

➤ Another Sicilian import, this shop has pastries that are as sweet as the owners are surly. But don't let the gruff manner dissuade you. Sicily is the thing here, so go cannoli, cassata, and anything with almonds. And for Carnevale don't miss their *sfince di San Giuseppe,* a massive choux pastry stuffed with sweetened whipped ricotta.

Regoli

Via dello Statuto 60

➤ Hands down, one of the best pastry shops in Rome. (See discussion on page 182.)

Innocenti

Via delle Luce 21

➤ This hard-to-find cookie shop is located on one of the back alleys of Trastevere. Before the neighborhood became known for its touristy nightlife, it was the center for small-scale productions like Innocenti, founded more than a hundred years ago. The white-capped ladies mix flour, sugar, and a handful of other ingredients to come up with more than 50 kinds of mouthwatering biscuits.

eating pastries in rome: new school

Andrea de Bellis

Piazza del Paradiso 56

➤ Andrea de Bellis, who used to provide pastries for some of Rome's best restaurants, has finally opened his own shop near Campo de' Fiori. Rich and elaborate modern cakes and pastries.

Cristalli di Zucchero

Via San Teodoro 88, 39-06-699-20945

➤ Cristalli di Zucchero has become one of the city's most popular stops to indulge in sophisticated pastries. Don't expect anything like a Roman, or even Italian, experience here. The exquisite pastries definitely come out of a French and northern European tradition. But the creative twists make their creations all their own. I always stop by on my way to the farmers' market next door.

Boccione

Via del Portico d'Ottavia 1

➤ The "Jewish Bakery."

recipes

When it comes to Italian pastries, I always leave the cooking to professionals. I've never attempted anything near creating a cannoli, *frappè,* or cassata. There is one

Italian pastry, though, that I think I do better than any Italian: the crostata. A crostata is the most basic and rustic of Italian tarts, and you can find them for sale in almost any bakery. The thing is, I think they are all pretty horrible. They are almost always made with margarine instead of real butter, and so the crust ends up tasting like cardboard. And even the homemade crostata I've had are so stingy when it comes to butter that they are just dry and almost always disappointing.

My secret, if you haven't already guessed, is butter, and good butter. Italian butter is the one thing I almost never buy, since it often has a slightly gamey taste to it. Instead, I prefer imported butter from Denmark, France, or Germany.

The traditional filling for a crostata is jam, such as the *crostata di marmalata* below, but I often make one that is filled with sweetened ricotta.

crostata di marmalata

Makes one 10-inch crostata

Crostata Crust
    1 cup (110 grams) all-purpose flour
    ½ cup (60 grams) whole wheat flour
    7 tablespoons (110 grams) unsalted
       butter, softened
    2 egg yolks, at room temperature
    ½ cup (100 grams) sugar
    Pinch of salt

Filling
    One jar of jam (about 1 cup)
    ⅓ cup chopped nuts (optional)

Preheat the oven to 350°F (180°C). Line a 10-inch tart pan with a removable bottom with parchment paper.

Put the flours into a large bowl, and make a well in center. Add the butter, egg yolks, sugar, and salt to the well. Mix the wet ingredients in the well with your fingers, then slowly start mixing in the flour. Just use your hand, and eventually the heel of your hand, to mush it all together until it forms a ball. This only takes a few minutes.

Let the dough rest for 10 minutes, then push it out into the prepared tart pan. Don't try to roll it out, just spread it out to the edges with the palm of your hand to form an even crust.

At this point the crust is ready for any jam filling. Empty out the jar (about 1 cup) of jam into the unbaked crust. Spread it out with the back of a spoon. Top with the nuts if using. Place on the middle rack of the oven and bake for about 25 minutes.

Let cool completely before serving.

ricotta, raspberry, and chocolate crostata

Makes one 10-inch crostata

- 1 recipe Crostata Crust (see previous recipe)
- 1½ cups fresh whole-milk ricotta
- ¾ cup (150 grams) sugar
- 1 large egg
- 2 cups fresh raspberries
- 1 cup chopped semisweet dark chocolate or chocolate chips

Preheat the oven to 350°F (180°C). Line a 10-inch tart pan with a removable bottom with parchment paper.

Place the crostata dough in the pan, spreading it out with the heel of your hand until it covers the bottom of the pan and a bit up the sides.

Bake the crust for about 15 minutes, or until it starts to turn golden. Remove from the oven and let cool. Leave the oven on.

Whip the ricotta with a fork until smooth. Add the sugar and egg and stir until incorporated and smooth. Fold in the berries and chocolate.

Fill the tart shell with the ricotta mixture, return it to the oven, and bake for about 25 minutes, or until set. Let cool to room temperature and serve.

the best time of day

Whenever I'm talking with friends or colleagues about how important it is to start off the day with a good breakfast, or the necessity of keeping the tradition of a family dinner alive, I'm full of personal stories, recipes, and examples. In my own home, I've always made an effort to get those two meals on the table, no matter everyone's hectic schedule. I admit, I'm as sanctimonious as the next person when it comes to embracing the family meal.

But when the discussion veers into the personal preference for breakfast or dinner, I quiet down. Some of my friends talk about making pancakes or porridge for the entire family every morning, while others talk about the joys of mapping out weeklong meal plans that enable them to get dinner on the table every single night.

But me? You want to know what my favorite meal of the day is? It's cocktail hour.

I know, you're thinking cocktail hour isn't really a meal. But in Italy, where every chance to drink and/or eat has a ritual attached to it, I've come to think of aperitivo time as the fourth meal of the day, as important for my sanity, health, and social life as any formal sit-down dinner party or healthy lunch.

One of the great things about mealtimes in Italy is that they are always social occasions. Families still gather around a table for lunch and dinner, and the whole fast-food, on-the-run thing has never really caught on. Most Italians would never think of eating alone, unless there was absolutely no other option available. Even the rapid-fire breakfast is a chance to stop by your favorite coffee bar and discuss the most recent governmental failure before you start your day.

While *pranzo* (lunch) and *cena* (dinner) are chances to chat and catch up on the day's events, the most social time of the day is, of course, aperitivo time. *Aperitivo* could be translated as "cocktail hour," since it's the time between a workday and dinner, and usually involves drinking something. But while in countries like the United States and the UK, alcohol, and getting buzzed, is an integral part of the equation, alcohol is not the major ingredient in this event.

It took me a while to understand the true meaning of *aperitivo*. The word itself should have given me a clue. *Aperitivo* means, literally, "opening up." At first I thought it was a reference to the start of a meal or an evening out, but, no. In this case the "opening up" refers to the digestive tract. Sorry to get so specific and physiological when you were probably hoping for a cocktail recipe or two (which will come, don't worry, further on), but first things first. Italians are always concerned about their digestion. If you ask Romans how they are doing, nine times out of ten the answer will involve some sort of report on their stomach and its workings.

Although having an aperitivo at a bar at the end of a workday with friends obviously has social appeal, there are also true, quasi-medical implications. Yes, in this case, cocktails can be good for you. The traditional drinks imbibed at this time of day—Negronis, Campari Sodas, Americanos—are made with bitters, and the mixtures of various herbs are intended to get the gastric juices flowing, stimulate the appetite, and get you ready for dinner to come. Because, god forbid, you wouldn't want to introduce your digestive tract to dinner with no warning.

Aperitivi are actually a relatively recent invention. It was Antonio Benedetto Carpano who supposedly invented the idea of the aperitivo in Torino in 1786. He can probably trace his inspiration back to the Middle Ages and into the Renaissance when people were mixing herbs and spices into wines for medicinal reasons (or, more likely, to improve the taste). But his vermouth, Carpano Antico, was one of the first of the fortified wines to mix herbs, spices, and sugar with wine to market a prepared drink meant specifically to precede a meal.

Eventually, the glass of vermouth turned into slightly more elaborate cocktails incorporating not only vermouth, but bitters and other spirits. After a while the word *aperitivo*, which referred to the drink itself, also came to mean to the ritual of meeting for a drink before a meal.

As with all things, aperitivo time has a bunch of rules to follow. First of all, it's not usually a long and drawn-out affair.

As with coffee, most people meet for an aperitivo at a bar, and stand at the counter while they are drinking. The whole idea of having an aperitivo was invented as something to do before a meal. And so originally there was minimal food involved. Just a bowlful of nuts or chips to provide the salty component to make you thirsty, as well as give some ballast for the minimal amount of alcohol. Traditionally the snack would be something like almonds or maybe a few olives. Weirdly, about fifteen years ago, processed snacks started making their appearance. Potato chips were the least offensive, with mixed pretzels coming in a close second. In fact, these prepackaged mixes of pretzels or nuts are so tied to the idea of aperitivi that they are displayed in a special section in supermarkets next to the bottles of vermouth and Campari, far away from wine and other spirits.

Lately, though, things have been looking better on the food front. The first aperitivi buffets appeared in Milan. For a fixed price you would get one drink, plus a chance to fill up your small plate at a buffet at the bar's counter. The idea took a while but has now caught on up and down Italy, with many bars offering pretty good spreads. Although they're not supposed to substitute for a real meal, the buffets have become so substantial that they often can stand in for a light dinner.

What to drink? Remember, alcoholic content is not the aim here. The point is to have a slightly alcoholic drink that will stimulate your appetite. So expect bitter. The main component of most of the traditional Italian aperitivi is Campari. At roughly 25 percent alcohol, it is meant to be mixed, and is never drunk straight. The bright red liqueur is probably the most famous of the Italian aperitivi. Invented in 1860 by Gaspare Campari in the north of Italy, its bright color originally came from the crushed shells of beetles. Don't worry, the recipe has since been changed, but the color remains, as does the distinctive bitter taste.

a glossary of classic italian cocktails

Campari and Soda. Although Campari is used as a base for other cocktails, its most popular form is in the prepackaged Campari Soda, which comes in darling conical bottles that were designed by futurist Fortunato Depero in 1932. While I'm partial to the little bottles (which make perfect bud vases), I usually end up mixing my own Campari soda to a strength slightly higher than the wimpy 10 percent that's marketed.

Americano. Supposedly this was one of the first cocktails served at Gaspare Campari's bar in Milan. A mix of Campari, red vermouth, and seltzer, it's a drink I have little use for, since it always seems like a wimpy Negroni. But a lot of my wimpy friends prefer it. It was originally called a

Milano/Torino, since the Campari is from Milan and the vermouth from Torino. At some point, around the 1900s, it was named after Americans, who seemed to order it a lot while in Europe, drinking it up during Prohibition.

Negroni. I love a cocktail that comes with a good story. Legend has it that in 1919 in Florence Count Camillo Negroni came into a bar and asked the bartender to add a little something to his Americano to give it more of a punch (my kind of guy). An ounce of gin, instead of the soda water, did the trick. Variations abound, with different bitters being substituted for the Campari. My favorite is the Cyn-Cyn, where the artichoke-based Cynar provides the bitter note. What the drink loses in its bright red color is made up for by its slightly smoother and sweeter taste.

Negroni Sbagliato. *Negroni Sbagliato* means "Mistaken Negroni." In this case the bartender makes the mistake of switching in a much lighter dose of prosecco in place of the gin. See? It's kind of like a Weight Watchers Negroni—at least that's what I tell myself.

Spritz. The spritz is a Venetian invention that has recently made its way south. It is traditionally made with prosecco and some sort of bitter liqueur like Campari, Aperol, or—if you happen to be in Venice—Select. The Spritz is not overly strong, and is

extremely thirst quenching, which makes it the perfect summertime cocktail. Also, the bright color of the Campari or Aperol renders the setting sun, shining through the rising bubbles, almost painfully pretty.

when in rome . . . aperitivo rules

- *Bitter is better:* There is a reason Italians invented the Negroni, Campari Soda, and Aperol Spritz. They all include bitters, which stimulate the appetite.

- *Get happy:* Many bars now offer special happy hour buffets. For about 7 to 10 euros, the price of a cocktail includes a plateful of nibbles that can substitute for dinner.

- *Timing:* Aperitivo is a before-meal event. Although midday aperitivi can happen between 12:00 and 1:00 p.m., most happen at the end of the day, between 6:00 and 8:00 p.m.

drinking with a view

In my mind, cocktails have one perfect garnish: a view. One definitely improves the other. While I live in Rome, and often take the city for granted, I realize that most of the world comes here for vacation—

and so are probably expecting views with their Negronis. Not surprisingly, many of the best bird's-eye-view perches are atop rooftop hotel bars. If you're thinking that this kind of experience is pricey, you're right. When it comes to these places, you are definitely paying for the real estate you are taking up. But since the best usually come with a high level of service and pitch-perfect aperitivi—I'm sometimes willing to pay the price.

Minerva Roof Garden

Hotel Minerva, Piazza della Minerva 69, 39-06-695-201

➤ This has got to be one of the most elegantly Roman drink/view combos in town: the rooftop of the Grand Hotel della Minerva. Located smack next to the Pantheon, the hotel bar takes up the best corner of the terrace. Get there by 7:00 p.m. and settle in for the spectacle of a Roman sunset.

Bar La Terazza

Hotel Eden, Via Ludovisi 49, 39-06-478-121

➤ While Negronis are not that hard to make (equal parts gin, vermouth, and Campari), I swear to god they just taste better when the rosy light of an October sunset in Rome comes streaming through them. And when the view is of the sunset over Roman gardens, and the Negronis are perfectly made, served in heavy glass tumblers by a white-jacketed waiter, well, it's hard to get any better than that. Perfectly made little canapés are included.

Hotel Forum

Via Tor de' Conti 25–30, 39-06-679-2446

➤ Located just at the edge of the Monti neighborhood, the Hotel Forum rises up just where Via Cavour ends at Fori Imperiali. The smallish cocktail terrace is reached by taking the elevator up to the top floor, walking through the restaurant, and up a narrow flight of stairs. Once reached, the pocket-size bar looks out over the Forum, and toward the Palatine and Campidoglio hills. As swallows swing by, order a Negroni or a Bellini, or even a gin and tonic, before you head on for dinner.

well-made cocktails

You can get an Italian aperitivo at almost any bar. But if you're looking for something a bit more creative and definitely well crafted, here are some places to start.

Barnum Café

Via del Pellegrino 87, 39-06-647-60483

➤ The comfortably funky and cozy bar is located just steps away from the more touristy Campo de' Fiori night scene. But instead of hawking fruit-flavored shots to junior-year-abroad students, Barnum's is well stocked with high-quality ingredients and bartenders who know how to mix them.

Caffè Propaganda

Via Claudia 15

➤ Located just a few blocks away from the Colosseum, Caffè Propaganda feels like a

New York meets Paris kind of bistro. The bar up front is large, perfectly designed, and one of the best places in the neighborhood to get anything from a classic martini (not an easy thing to find in Rome) to a pitch-perfect Negroni.

Bar Locarno

Via della Penna 22, 39-06-361-0841

➢ From spring through summer their shady courtyard is a relaxing place to settle in for a drink and some snacks. In wintertime nothing beats sitting by their open working fireplace in their art nouveau salon. It seems a bit pricey—14 euros for a cocktail—but this includes a plate of finger food, which can almost make a meal. Coconut-battered shrimp, mini meatballs, and seafood salad are all delicious

recipes

While it's relatively easy to get a well-made Negroni, Americano, or Spritz at almost any bar in Rome, going beyond these well-loved classics can be hazardous. Although things are starting to change, and a few skilled mixologists are spreading their gospel, it's much more common to come across badly made Mojitos and Margaritas when venturing beyond anything Campari based, which is why I took a good hard look at the Italian liquor cabinet and began to experiment at home. I wanted to develop cocktails that were informed not only by the classic ingredients such as Campari and vermouth, but also by other weird and wonderful bottles. Rose-infused liquor from Puglia, artichoke-packed Cynar, the dozens of unique *amari* that are made throughout Italy.

But I also wanted to work in the fresh and seasonal tastes and textures that define Italy. The green smell of basil, ripe tomatoes from Naples, and briny olives from Gaeta. Rosemary and thyme, oranges and lemons, even truffles were fair game.

the mostardini

Serves 1

I grew up in a family that mythologized *bollito misto*. It was one of those dishes that we constantly talked about, and planned on having whenever a festive occasion presented itself. New Year's was always a sure bet.

Recently I was daydreaming about bollito. But then I realized that what I was actually craving were the traditional condiments that accompany the boiled meats, *salsa verde* and *frutta mostarda*. Salsa verde, a heavenly mix of parsley, garlic, and lemon, takes some preparation. But frutta mostarda? I actually had a jar of that in the fridge, and realized I didn't need the bollito as an excuse to crack the lid.

And then the miracle occurred. Or

(continued)

was it an epiphany? Whatever. As I was digging into the spicy, syrupy goodness of the mostarda I had a thought: cocktail ingredient!

I use flavored syrups all the time for cocktails. And here I was with a jar of sweet and spicy syrup studded with jewel-like pieces of fruit just asking me to mix it into something. OK, I know a lot of you out there don't like it when the word *martini* is bastardized. So I'm not calling this a martini, but a completely different name: Mostardini. That OK?

> **2½ ounces vodka**
> **½ ounce sweet white vermouth**
> **1½ tablespoons frutta mostarda syrup**
> **Ice**
> **3 small pieces frutta mostarda**

Pour the vodka into a shaker. Add the vermouth and syrup. Add ice and stir (don't shake) until well chilled. Strain into a chilled martini glass. Garnish with pieces of frutta mostarda skewered onto a toothpick.

martini sporco

Serves 1

I go through phases. There was my quilting phase. There was my knitting phase. And last spring, my dirty martini phase. For some reason that was the only

thing I wanted to drink. Vodka, a hint of extra-dry vermouth, and a bit of brine from the olive jar. For a while, I Frenched things up, switching in Lillet for the Martini & Rossi. But the final touch, always: three pimento-stuffed green olives.

Pimento-stuffed green olives? By far the most industrially produced condiment in my fridge. It dawned on me that maybe I didn't have to use these hard little pitted nubbins from who knows where. (And what's with those "pimentos"?) I had at least five other kinds of olives on hand, bought at the farmers' market, so why not try to use those? I decided to skip the whole brine thing. But I figured to get a true olive taste going (which is what you want, right?), all I had to do was muddle the hell out of the little things.

The martini turned out just how I imagined it tasting. The rich, strong taste that we all love in Italian olives came shining through. I don't think anyone will describe the cloudy, olive-infused vodka as pretty. (You certainly can't picture Don Draper sipping one.) But the olives on the toothpick that had sat in my drink for a half an hour? Divine.

> **2 large good-quality Italian olives in brine, with the pits**
> **4 small black oven-dried olives, with the pits**
> **2½ ounces vodka**

(continued)

1 tablespoon Martini & Rossi extra-dry
    vermouth
Ice

Carefully pit the olives, both kinds, trying
not to destroy them.

In a shaker, place 1 brined olive and
2 black olives and add the vodka. Muddle
well, mashing up those olives as best you
can. Add the vermouth and ice and stir,
to chill. Slip the remaining olives onto a
toothpick, and place in a martini glass
(chilled if you like).

Carefully pour the contents of the
shaker into the glass, using a fine sieve to
keep out the olive bits.

positano gin and tonic

Serves 1

There are a lot of reasons that Gillian
and I are friends. Although we met
through Twitter, we are now neighbors in
Rome and, of course, proximity breeds
friendship. And while we share interests
like blogging, food, travel, and offspring,
our friendship is based on something
much deeper. Yes, I'm talking about
cocktails. So when Gillian hosted me in
Positano recently, of course she made
sure cocktails were on the itinerary. While
I'm usually the one mixing things up, I love
it when friends take over. Besides it being
enjoyable, I always learn something new.
Gillian did not disappoint. She took the

basic idea of a gin and tonic, and turned it
into something very Positano-ish. Lemons
of course, but also a lot of fresh basil and
slices of cool cucumber. The addition of
supersize ice cubes was a nice touch,
especially in a land that usually frowns
on ice. So was the incredible view of the
Amalfi coast, which is, I'm sorry to say,
the one element of this drink you are not
going to be able to re-create at home.

1 lemon wedge
1 slice cucumber
3 fresh basil leaves
2 ounces gin (Hendrick's is best)
Ice
Tonic water
1 slice cucumber and sprig of basil for
    garnish

In a rocks glass, muddle the lemon,
cucumber, and basil. Add the gin. Add ice
and top with tonic water. Stir, garnish with
a slice of cucumber and a sprig of basil,
and serve, preferably while looking out
over the Positano bay.

what to eat

I've taken the whole idea of the aperitivo
buffet to heart. I love the idea of laying out
an entire tableful of food I've prepared
ahead of time, so that everyone can just eat
as they sip at their Negronis. As is done at
the buffets found in most bars, I tend toward the carbohydrate side of things (all

the better to absorb the drinks). Bruschetta are my favorite canvas to work with. When you say "bruschetta" (or, as my mother says, "brushetta"), most people immediately think tomatoes. And I agree, it's hard to beat grilled bread topped with August tomatoes, and maybe a bit of salt and olive oil. But bruschetta can be so much more. Anything, in fact.

On a base of toasted bread, I can pretty much layer on almost anything from cheese to vegetables to cured meats.

much will depend on how salty your pancetta is) and pepper. Cook over high heat until browned and tender. Return the pancetta, with its juices, to the pan and stir to distribute.

Toast the bread, over an open fire if possible. If not, then over the flames of your stovetop, or in a toaster.

While the bread is still hot, rub it with the garlic clove and drizzle with a bit of olive oil. Divide the zucchini mixture among the slices of bread and serve.

bruschetta with zucchini and pancetta

Makes 6 bruschette

½ cup cubed pancetta

3 medium zucchini, diced

Salt

Freshly ground black pepper

6 slices crusty Italian bread, cut about ½ inch thick

1 garlic clove, peeled

Extra-virgin olive oil, for drizzling

Place a medium frying pan over medium heat. Add the pancetta and cook, until it has rendered its fat and become crisp. Using a slotted spoon, remove the pancetta from the fat and transfer it to a small bowl—not a paper towel. You want to retain all that good pork fat!

Add the zucchini to the rendered fat in the pan and stir. Sprinkle with salt (how

asparagus ricotta bruschetta

Makes 4 bruschette

1 small bunch wild asparagus (or pencil-thin asparagus)

2 tablespoons extra-virgin olive oil

1 small garlic clove, chopped

Salt

6 stalks steamed asparagus

⅓ cup fresh whole-milk ricotta

Freshly ground black pepper

4 slices crusty Italian bread

Cut the wild asparagus into 1-inch pieces.

Heat 1 tablespoon of the olive oil in a small pan over low heat. Add the garlic and cook for 1 minute. Add the wild asparagus, and cook just until tender enough to eat, about 4 minutes or so. Season with salt to taste. Set aside.

(continued)

In a small food processor, blend the steamed asparagus, ricotta, the remaining 1 tablespoon of olive oil, and salt and pepper to taste.

Toast the bread.

Divide the ricotta mixture evenly among the bread slices. Top each with the wild asparagus.

Although the asparagus version of this recipe is fantastic, feel free to experiment. I'm thinking peas, fava beans, zucchini, and even green beans would be delicious. (And no, Mom, leftover salad is not going to work.)

fava and pecorino bruschetta

Makes 6 bruschette

A traditional meal for May 1 (Labor Day in Italy) includes fresh fava beans and pecorino cheese. It's a very social kind of snack, since everyone peels their own fava beans, nibbling on them raw, while they alternate with bits of cheese. It tastes great, and a pile of fava beans on the table is admittedly gorgeous. But I always find it a bit too rustic a combo to serve at a real meal. Plus, I'm always thinking that there must be a way to incorporate a bit of salt and olive oil, which I feel are missing. So I decided to take the idea of springtime *fave e pecorino*, and turn it into a bruschetta.

A word about the pecorino: *Pecorino* is simply the Italian word for "sheep's milk cheese," which covers quite a range of textures and tastes. Pecorino Romano can be sharp and salty, while Pecorino Toscano is definitely more nutty tasting. In this dish I used a rather fresh cheese that I had picked up earlier in the day at the local *caseificio*. So if possible, you want to find a cheese that is on the softer side, not too hard. More or less the same texture as the raw fava beans, and not overly aged.

> 2 pounds (1 kilo) fava beans in their pods
> 3 tablespoons extra-virgin olive oil, plus more for drizzling
> Salt
> Freshly ground black pepper
> 6 slices crusty Italian bread
> 1 garlic clove (optional)
> 1 cup cubed pecorino cheese (see headnote)

Remove the fava beans from their shells, but leave the outer skin on the beans. Roughly chop with a mezzaluna or knife.

Place the beans in a bowl, toss with the 3 tablespoons of olive oil, and season with salt and pepper.

Toast the bread, over a fire if possible.

Rub the toasted bread with a piece of peeled garlic if desired. Drizzle lightly with olive oil and sprinkle with salt. Top each slice with some of the chopped fava beans and then some of the cubed pecorino. Drizzle with a bit more olive oil, and top with more freshly ground black pepper.

counting in italian

have a hard time with numbers. I was never any good at math, I'm always messing up on dates, and if you tell me your phone number I will forget it in the time it takes to grab a pen. This also probably explains why I'm not a great baker. Baking takes a precision and attention to quantities and weights that I just don't have.

Moving to Italy didn't help much. I'm still at a loss when someone tells me it is 22 degrees Celsius. Is that hot or cold? Do I need a sweater or a coat? I've finally memorized that 350 degrees Fahrenheit is 180 degrees Celsius, but only because I've had to look it up 457,000 times over the last twenty years.

And I have to admit that there are a few other measurements I've learned over my years of cooking in Italy that have gone a long way toward curing my habit to overbuy. 100 grams seems to be a pretty steady indicator of portion size: 100 grams of pasta per person; 100 grams of meat. Because nothing is prepackaged when I go to the market in Italy, I always have to specify exactly how much I'd like to have.

I learned this the hard way. When I would finally manage to get to the front of the line at the vegetable stand, I would very clearly ask for some apples. Only to have the fruttivendolo look at me with raised eyebrows. So I would repeat it again, that I'd like some apples, please. Finally she would take pity on me and ask, *"Quante mele?"* ("How many apples?") "Oh, four or five!" I'd reply, thinking that by now we'd cleared everything up, but, no. She wanted even more specificity. *"Mezzo kilo?"* ("Half a kilo?") Like how was I supposed to know how much the apples weighed? Wasn't she the one with the scale?

For a while I thought it was just my mother-in-law, who is particularly fixated on numbers. Whenever we chatted on the phone, our main topic of conversation would be, of course, what I was cooking. If I told her that I was having a dinner party and was making, say, a pork roast, her first question would be for how many people. Then she would sort of mumble to herself and say something like *"Allora, deve prendere un arrosto di 3.6 kili."* ("So, you have to get a pork roast of 3.6 kilos.") It was always very specific, and always involved some sort of math equation that was a mystery to me.

When I took the time to listen to everyone else though, not just at the fruit and vegetable stand, but also at the bakery, the butcher's, and the fish store, I realized that everyone was being very specific about measurements.

Eventually, after years of hearing these formulas over and over, I finally got the hang of it. I could now shop like a pro, figuring out not only how much meat and pasta to buy and prepare, but everything down to the last leaf of lettuce.

Which is why, I learned, Italians don't usually have leftovers. There is no such thing as a doggie bag when you go to an Italian restaurant. The portions that are so carefully measured out in the kitchen are exactly the portions that can be easily eaten by one person at one meal. When my Italian friends see my hoard of Tupperware, which falls on my head from the cabinet above the sink every time I open it, they have no idea what it is for.

The strange thing is, though, all this attention to precise measurements when shopping for food gets thrown out the window the minute you ask someone for a recipe. My mother-in-law, who is so precise in measuring out the main ingredient of her dish—be it pasta, meat, fruit, or vegetable—is completely vague in recounting recipes. *"Ci metta un po di olio . . .* you put a little olive oil in the pan . . ." begins most of the recipes I've ever learned from her. But if I ask her exactly how much oil, it's as if I'm speaking another language. "Didn't you hear me? A little." As if that is some sort of standard measurement not to be confused with *molto* (a lot) or *pochissimo* (very, very little).

Italian cookbooks even have a technical abbreviation for this tendency to vagueness: QB. It took me the longest time to realize that QB, when added onto an ingredient, meant *quanto basta*, as much as you need. And really, it makes perfect sense. Because who knows how much oil you may need or want in any given recipe? Or salt, for that matter. Or just about anything else. As with

most things Italian, everyone has his or her own opinion, and when it comes to cooking, to each his own.

recipes

Italians are very good at making just enough food for the meal at hand. Rarely do they go way overboard with Tupperware containers full of leftovers clogging the fridge after a meal. But on that rare occasion when they do have a bit of pasta left over from a family meal, it often makes its way into this rustic frittata, which is pure heaven.

Although you can certainly make this frittata with pasta that already has a sauce on it, I love it made when the noodles are barely dressed with a bit of olive oil. That way I can add handfuls of Parmigiano and pecorino, for a very cheesy and chewy dish. The trick is making the pasta the star of the show, with just enough eggs to bind it all together.

And while frittatas can be eaten piping hot, I like this one served at room temperature, as do most Italians. Although I have served this up as the main course for a dinner party on Sunday, this dish made from leftover pasta is even better as a leftover itself. A thick slice between two pieces of bread is the perfect beach picnic food or even breakfast the next day.

frittata di pasta

Makes one 10-inch frittata; serves 4 to 5

3 cups cooked pasta

Extra-virgin olive oil, as needed

6 large eggs

¾ cup grated Parmigiano-Reggiano cheese

½ cup cubed aged sheep's milk cheese

½ cup chopped fresh flat-leaf parsley

Salt

Freshly ground black pepper

If you don't have any leftover pasta, cook and drain the pasta and toss it with a tablespoon or so of olive oil.

Crack the eggs into a large mixing bowl, and stir with a fork to break up. Add the cheeses and stir well to mix. Add the pasta and parsley, season with salt and pepper, and stir to combine.

Heat a 10-inch (60-cm) nonstick frying pan with enough olive oil to coat the bottom in a thin layer. Add the egg and pasta mixture, and use a wooden spoon to spread it evenly over the pan.

Cover with a flat lid, and let cook over low heat until set, about 10 minutes. If the top is still runny, hold the pan and lid carefully together and flip it over. Then slide the frittata back into the hot pan to finish cooking the top, which is now the bottom.

You can serve this hot, but it's even better at room temperature. In any case, let it rest at least 5 minutes before cutting into wedges and serving.

picchiapò

Serves 5

While Italians don't usually have leftovers, there is a tradition in cucina povera of making one ingredient last over several meals. For instance, coda alla vaccinara is oxtail cooked in tomato sauce. The oxtail will be the main course for one meal, while the rich beef-flavored sauce will be served on top of pasta the next day. The same is true of boiled beef. A big piece of beef would be used to make *brodo*. Not only would the brodo be used to cook pasta in for one meal, but also the beef could often then be stretched for at least another two meals. The Roman version of bollito helper is called *picchiapò*. If you think the name *picchiapò* sounds strange, it does. No one is quite sure how this dish got its name. But it is certainly fun to say "pee-ke-ya-po," not to mention the dish is good to eat.

I realize that leftover boiled beef isn't something that a lot of people have to deal with. Although traditional picchiapò calls for boiled beef, I'm thinking that this recipe would work for any kind of leftover meat you may have. Yes, even that turkey you stuck in the freezer last November.

1 pound (½ kilo) leftover boiled beef
1 large white onion
2 celery stalks
Extra-virgin olive oil, as needed
2 cups canned tomatoes
Salt
Freshly ground black pepper

Pull the boiled beef into bite-size pieces. Cut the onion in half, and slice it into thin rings.

Slice the celery on the diagonal into ¼-inch slices.

In a pan large enough to hold everything, warm the oil over medium heat. Reduce the heat to low, add the onion and celery, and cook, stirring, for about 25 minutes. You want them to soften, but not brown. Add the tomatoes. Increase the heat to medium, and cook for another 10 minutes. Stir in the beef, cover, and simmer for 20 minutes. Season with the salt and pepper.

Serve with mashed potatoes, or a loaf of crusty bread to sop up all the juices.

how to eat pizza like a roman

One of my very first memories of being in Rome involves pizza.

When we moved to Rome after my parents' whirlwind decision, my father hadn't made any plans beyond reserving a couple of hotel rooms through a travel agent he knew in St. Louis. As we piled out of the taxi from the airport, on that torrid August day, even I could tell that this was not the Rome my father had been describing to me and my sisters during the two weeks leading up to our trip. Set somewhere on the outskirts of Rome, in some modern neighborhood, the Caesar Augustus Hotel was, within five minutes of our stepping into our stifling room, declared "the Caesar Disgustus" by me and my sisters, all cranky and jet-lagged from our first transatlantic trip.

We soon passed out from jet lag and exhaustion. I was the first to wake up. In my disoriented state I couldn't quite remember where I was, but I knew one thing: I was starved. While my mother and two little sisters were still sleeping soundly, my father saw me starting to stir and came over quietly and whispered in my ear: "Do you want to go get a pizza sandwich?"

This was my first inkling that things were not as "Disgustus" as they seemed. Even though I didn't know what it was, just the idea of a pizza sandwich was enough to make me view things differently. As I slipped on my clogs (yes, this was the '70s), and got ready to sneak out the door with my father, I had one doubt. What if he was making it up? My family had been known to invent improbable foods to torture each other. I will forever remember the time my parents took my sisters to a restaurant without me and they all came back swearing they had enjoyed huge plates of chocolate spaghetti. Could a pizza sandwich be something my dad just invented to keep me quiet for the few moments it took to get me out of the room so I wouldn't wake the others?

We made our way out onto the hot sidewalk and crossed the street to a coffee bar. When we walked in I saw a glass case full of sandwiches. None of them looked like any pizza I knew. But my dad had obviously become some sort of expert during the few days he had spent in Rome the previous month, since he knew just what to ask for. "Pizza bianca," he said while pointing to a large square sandwich. After heating it up in a sandwich press, the bar man handed it to me, wrapped in a paper-thin napkin.

"See," my dad explained, "here in Rome they bake pizza dough plain, then slice it open to use as a sandwich." And in fact, it was pizza dough, sliced down the middle and stuffed with what I soon learned was mortadella. It was my first taste of Rome and my first realization that things I knew back home, like pizza or pasta, were to be much more complicated and, of course, better and more delicious. SpaghettiOs would soon be replaced by *spaghetti al pomodoro*,

and I learned that not all ravioli is breaded, deep-fried, and served with a dipping sauce (a St. Louis specialty, in case you didn't know).

While the "pizza sandwich" from my first meal in Italy became a much-loved favorite over our two years living in Rome, it was only decades later, when I moved back to Italy full time as a graduate student in Florence, that I realized that my favorite way of eating pizza was peculiar to Rome. In Florence I was able to get spongy focaccia in any manner of ways, but I could never seem to recapture that crisp yet chewy dough I remembered from Rome, stuffed with a thin slice of porky mortadella. As it turns out, what I thought was just a common kind of sandwich was, in fact, a Roman specialty: *pizza e mortazza*.

Pizza, I learned, like everything else in Italy, is intensely regional. Even the names for different kinds of dough changes from region to region, and parsing out the differences between Ligurian *focaccia*, Tuscan *shciacciata,* and Roman *pizza bianca* was a delicious confusion.

Although Naples is considered to be the birthplace of pizza, Rome has its own very distinctive and delicious pizza culture. But before diving in, it helps to have some sort of knowledge of the different kinds.

Pizza. When people in Rome say they are going out for dinner to have a pizza they mean round, single-serving pizzas. These are made to order by specially trained *pizzaioli* in *pizzerias*, almost always in a wood-burning oven. Most pizzerias are only open in the evenings, for dinner (although there are some notable and recent exceptions to this rule).

Pizza al Taglio. This is sheet pizza, sold mostly by the piece in small storefronts that specialize in this type of pizza. It is sold by the weight and has various toppings. You can either buy it to take away or, more commonly, eat it standing up at a counter.

Pizza Bianca. This is the white pizza dough that I bit into on my first morning in Rome. It is white dough, with a drizzle of olive oil, that has been baked on high heat. It is often sold in bakeries, and is meant to be eaten right away while hot, and is one of Rome's true street foods.

Every Roman has their favorite pizzeria. While their choice has a lot to do with taste, of course, it also has as much to do with location. Just like having a favorite neighborhood bar, all Romans have their favorite corner pizza joint.

This is where they head on a Sunday night when the family feels like going out for an inexpensive meal. Or the place where they stop on the way home from work during the week for a pizza to go. And, in fact, as you walk around about 8:00 p.m. in a residential neighborhood, you'll see folks walking home with a boxed pizza. These dependable, local places rarely get written up in guidebooks or blogs. Mostly because they aren't doing anything beyond the norm: good pizzas cooked to order in a wood-burning oven.

I have to admit to having a blind spot when it comes to my own neighborhood pizzeria. We decided to go there recently, and I was all set to call up to reserve. I got out my iPhone, opened my own app *Eat Rome*, only to realize that I hadn't included Alle Carrette. I'd included all the "artisan" trendy pizza places like Gatta Mangiona, Sforno, and Pizzarium. I'd even included some neighborhood places from across town, like Ivo's, but no Alle Carrette.

There's no reason, except that I take this very good pizzeria completely for granted. It's been there since I moved into the neighborhood twenty years ago, and almost all the waiters and certainly the *pizzaiolo* are still the same. They've been feeding my daughters since they could first gnaw on a crust.

Alle Carrette is typical of a good local Roman pizzeria. The dough is left to rise overnight, then rolled out superthin. The wood-burning oven is huge and its high temperature means that they can turn out pizzas fast and furiously. Toppings are for the most part traditional. You're not going to find any pumpkin or balsamic reduction here. Instead, this is where I order a *Capriciosa*, which in Rome means "pizza with prosciutto, mushrooms, artichoke hearts, olives, and a hard-boiled egg." Sophie almost always orders the high-end version of a *pizza Margherita*, with mozzarella di bufala and *pachino* tomatoes, while Emma orders the Marinara topped with *rughetta*. Domenico—being the southern boy that he is—goes for the calzone.

Although it seems counterintuitive to start out a pizza meal with deep-fried appetizers, called fritti, this is exactly what Romans do. A batter-dipped piece of baccalà, "salt cod," is the most common. Since it's meant to be eaten with your hands, it is served with a protective paper napkin so you don't burn your fingers on the piping hot fish. In season, we'll also order a plateful of fried zucchini flowers, stuffed with bits of anchovies and mozzarella.

Almost no one drinks wine with pizza. This is the time for something fizzy and a tall glass of *birra alla spina*, usually Peroni or Moretti, is what most people order.

when in rome . . . eating pizza

1. *There is no sharing:* In sit-down pizzerias each person orders their own single-serving-size pizza.

2. *Use a fork and knife:* In Rome, at sit-down pizzerias, this is the way it's done.

3. *Olio santo:* Don't go looking for a shaker of dried red pepper flakes or oregano.

The only condiment that's available is *olio santo,* a bottle of hot pepper–infused olive oil.

4. *Red versus white:* Most pizzerias will divide the menu in half: bianco or rosso. *Rosso* means "red," and the pizzas comes with tomato sauce. *Bianco* means "white," and the pizzas come with either mozzarella or no cheese at all, but never tomato sauce.

where to eat pizza in rome

Dinner: Traditionally pizzerias in Rome are open only in the evenings. Although this is starting to change, for now most of the best pizzerias—new and old—are dinnertime affairs. When I go out for pizza in Rome, convenience often trumps quality. Many of the best, most innovative pizzerias are located in neighborhoods outside of the center of town. That said, they are worth the effort to get there. But then my local is nothing to turn up your nose at.

Gatta Mangiona
Via Ozanam 30–32, 39-06-534-6702
➤ Considered by many to be the best pizzeria in Rome. This is a Roman take on Neapolitan.

Located in the residential Monteverde neighborhood, they do have a menu, but better to look on the blackboard for the daily

specials, which are also online, so you can arrive prepared. Toppings include things like creamy Gorgonzola, pumpkin, herring, and balsamic reduction and the other with cherry tomatoes, cubes of *primo sale,* and puntarelle. Start out with a selection of their daily fritti.

Sforno

Via Statilio Ottato 114, 39-06-715-46118

➤ Many swear that Sforno currently makes the best pizza in Rome. The only reason some people never make it there is its out-of-the-way location in the Tuscolana neighborhood. But if you are in Rome for the pizza, then hop on the metro or grab a taxi. Like many of the new generation of boutique pizzerias in Rome, Sforno has crusts that are on the thick and puffy side, more Neapolitan than Roman. One of their most famous pizzas is The Greenwich: mozzarella, Stilton, and a port reduction. I love their Cacio e Pepe precut into slices, with a pepper mill in the center for laying it on.

La Fucina

Via Giuseppe Lunati 25, 39-06-559-3368

➤ La Fucina is known for a few things, including the superb quality of their pizzas and the inventive toppings they layer on. But these two things definitely come at a price. La Fucina is also known for the more-than-usual cost of their pizzas: 22 to 34 euros per pizza. It starts to make more sense once you get there. First of all, the pizzas are big, and made to be split. And another completely unique thing about La Fucina is that you decide on several pizzas for the entire table, and then the owner decides in which order they should be served. They then start to come to the table, one after the other, each taking its turn. Each pizza is already sliced into eight neat and tidy servings. The toppings are inventive, seasonal, and usually involve copious amounts of vegetables and pork. La Fucina is located outside of the historic center of Rome.

Pizzeria Leoncino

Via del Leoncino 28, 39-06-686-7757

➤ It's hard to find a good pizzeria that is open for lunch. Also, the area in the center of Rome (between the Pantheon and the Spanish Steps) makes this even more of a challenge. This place is both centrally located and open at lunch. It is very much an old-fashioned neighborhood place, its specialty pizza with onions, beans, and sausage.

Alle Carrette

Via Madonna dei Monti 95, 39-06-679-2770

➤ Located in Monti, this is just a local pizza place, which is very, very good. Expect a pizza with a thin Roman crust. Every neighborhood has a good pizza place; this is ours. They have recently started opening for lunch as well as dinner, and have a nice outside terrace in the summer.

Pizza a Taglio: This pizza by the slice is available all day long, so it's great for a late-morning snack or a picnic kind of lunch.

Pizzarium

Via della Meloria 43, 39-06-3974-5416

➤ Pizzarium has become a mecca for foodies in Rome, and its creator, Gabriele Bonci, their god. This would all be pretty weird sounding, except that the pizza he turns out is nothing short of miraculous. This is not a pizzeria, but a pizza al taglio place. In other words, the pizzas come out in large trays, and you buy slices to eat standing up (or you can take it out). Bonci is so revered because he has single-handedly reinvented this unique form of Roman street food. His reworking of the formula for creating the dough has resulted in a worldwide following. Light and airy, it supports a unique symphony of toppings.

La Renella

Via del Moro 15, 39-06-581-7265

➤ Known for their large loaves of rustic bread, they are also the makers of some of the best-loved pizza by the slice in Trastevere. Almost always open.

Roscioli

Via dei Chiavari 34, 39-06-686-4045

➤ The most famous bakery in Rome? Many say so. Yes, fantastic bread, but also amazing pizza by the slice, including what some consider to be the best pizza bianca in town.

Forno di Campo de' Fiori

Piazza Campo de' Fiori 22, 39-06-6880-6662

➤ One of the oldest bakeries in town. Fresh, hot pizza bianca all day long, which you can watch being made through their storefront workshop window.

recipes

gabriele bonci's pizza

Serves 8

In 2011 I had the great good fortune to attend a series of pizza classes with Gabriele Bonci. His pizza al taglio, sold at the pocket-size Pizzarium, had become an essential meal on anyone's trip to Rome. Since Gabriele is dedicated to spreading the gospel of well-made pizza, he decided to teach how to re-create his pizza at home in a domestic oven. The series of posts I wrote on my blog about my experiences in these first classes, and subsequent ones I attended, have been among my most popular. Here follows his original recipe, but for a complete experience visit my Youtube channel, where you will begin to understand the unique way in which this Michelangelo of pizza handles his dough.

> 8 cups (2.2 pounds/1 kilo) tipo 0 or tipo 1 flour, preferably Burrato from Mulino Marino

(continued)

2½ teaspoons (7 grams) active dry instant
  yeast
3⅓ cups (700 grams/700 milliliters) water
1 tablespoon plus 1 teaspoon (20 grams)
  fine sea salt
3 tablespoons (40 grams/45 milliliters)
  extra-virgin olive oil

Mix the flour, yeast, and water in a large bowl, using a spoon. When it is almost mixed, and the lumps are mostly gone, add the salt, and then the oil. It will seem very wet; don't be scared; the wetter the dough, the better.

Flip the dough out onto a lightly floured surface and knead it gently by folding the dough in half, over itself, toward you. Grab the dough by the two corners facing you, and pick it up like an envelope, turn it 90 degrees, and place it back on the floured board. Repeat this motion a few times, without really kneading the dough. Fold and turn, fold and turn. It will seem very sticky at first, but when you get the hang of it, it gets easier.

Transfer the dough to a lightly oiled bowl and let it rest for another 15 minutes. Do this two or three more times. This is the step that Bonci calls "regenerating the dough." Don't overknead. In fact, don't knead at all. By the third time, the dough will be springy and not sticky. This process will take about an hour or so.

When this is done, return the dough to the bowl, cover very tightly, and let rise in the fridge for 24 hours.

Take the dough out of the fridge and let it come to room temperature. Preheat the oven to the hottest setting it has: 480°F (250°C).

Lightly flour a board and follow these directions to get your dough into your oiled pan. The important thing is not to be violent with the dough! (My friend Judy got yelled at in class for being too violent.) In fact, the first day we all overworked our dough, and ended up with flat pizzas that cooked unevenly and even burned (yes, that includes you, Judy). What you want to do is be very gentle, massage the dough, and seek to retain the pockets of air that have formed overnight.

Place one ball of dough, about 12 ounces (350 grams), onto the floured surface. Using your fingertips, gently stretch out the dough into roughly the shape of your 12 x 20-inch rectangular pan. Once you have formed your rough shape, turn it so that a short end is facing you. Stretch your left arm across the dough, diagonally, so that your left hand is gently touching the top of the rectangle. Using your right hand, carefully pick up the lower right-hand corner of the rectangle and fold it over your left arm. As you raise your left arm, palm

(continued)

down, swing your right arm underneath to support the rest of the dough, palm down. You should now have the entire rectangle draped across your two arms, palms down. Gently widen your arms to stretch the dough into your pan.

This is one of those things that sound incredibly complicated (and it is, kind of), but once you do it a few times you get the hang of it.

Don't worry about fancy toppings at this point. Master the dough first and then you can worry about getting creative with toppings. For now, either top with tomatoes: just imported pelati, with a bit of olive oil and salt added, or else just with olive oil and salt.

Place the pan on the floor of your oven. Each oven will bake differently, so you have to experiment. If you have a baking stone, all the better. It is important to get your oven as hot as possible.

After the pizza has been in the oven for about 15 minutes, check to see if the bottom is baking. Take it out and lift up the crust and take a peek underneath. If it seems like it's almost done, move it to the center rack and bake until finished, about another 10 minutes.

Take the pizza out of the oven, remove it from the pan immediately, and let it cool on the rack.

IMPORTANT NOTE: Bonci kept repeating, over and over and over, that the recipe

was really only about 10 percent of the success (or failure) of a pizza. It was all in the handling of the dough—in the *manipolazione.* And in fact, the pizzas we made the first evening, before we knew what we were doing (with dough that had been made in advance by the master himself), came out flat, and sad and burned. But once we all learned the trick of handling the dough—or rather, not handling it too much—our pizzas were light and fluffy and something we could be proud of. A big help in the entire process is, of course, taking a course with Bonci himself. If you can't make it to Rome, then visit my blog, where you'll find many videos showing him in action. Watch the videos, then watch them a few more times. You'll get it eventually.

topping your pizza alla bonci

So the procedure is as follows:

- **Make the dough.**
- **Let it rise.**
- **Lay the dough in the pan.**
- **Drizzle with oil, or top with a very thin layer of tomatoes (see note).**
- **Bake.**
- **Let cool slightly.**
- **Top!**

And the added extra-cool bonus of this method? You can bake the crusts ahead of time, and finish them off at the last minute for your pizza party. Makes you want to try this at home, right?

So, on to the toppings. Some of the toppings are added to the cooled, then reheated pizza, and left as is, without a trip back into the oven. Some, including cheeses, make a trip back to the oven just until the cheese melts, and are then finished with other ingredients that will remain uncooked. It's all up to you.

This is where you can let your imagination run wild. But even Bonci has some rules. For instance, never use more than three toppings. "That's a balanced pizza," he says. "Anything more would be too much."

The ingredients: Does it go without saying that you should use the best possible toppings for your pizza? The mozzarella should be the best you can get, and if you can get a *treccia* (braid)

this is the best consistency for pizza (less watery). Do not go to all this trouble to make the dough, only to top it with less than extraordinary ingredients. This is the place to use your goat cheese caciotta, the coppa you got from Abruzzo, the baby spinach from the farmers' market.

And do think about colors. There is a reason certain foods look good together. "Take mozzarella, tomatoes, and basil," mused Bonci. "Sure, they look good together, but they also perfectly balance creaminess, acidity, and freshness. Tastes follow colors naturally."

Note: There is reason behind this method, of course. First of all, the crust isn't burdened with heavy toppings, and so remains crisp, airy, and light. No watery mozzarella weighing things down. No ethereal bits of prosciutto getting burned.

{ chapter 24 }

learning to love grappa

love having people over for dinner. I adore the entire process of shopping, cooking, and setting the table, and then enjoying the meal. But I get really excited at the end of the meal, when we get to the after-dinner drinks. "Anyone want a grappa?" And sure enough, at least one (if not most) of my guests says, "No, I hate grappa." So I bring out the bottles of amaro, limoncello (yuck!), and even cognac. But I also bring out at least three bottles of grappa. But not just any grappa. It's Nonino grappa and, since the bottles are so distinctive (much classier and elegant than anything else on the table), they are the first things that get my guests' attention.

"Well, OK . . . I guess I'll try some." And usually, all it takes is one sip and they are grappa converts. As it turns out, the grappa they've tried up until now has almost nothing to do with what I serve.

I can understand their hesitation. Even though much has changed in the world of grappa in the last decade or so, most of the grappa out there is still dreck. That there is even any attempt at producing artisanally crafted grappas and aquavits in Italy is almost entirely due to the Nonino family, whom I had the pleasure of getting to know about twelve years ago when I wrote a feature about them. I have been a huge supporter (and, I admit it, drinker) ever since.

A bit of background: Traditionally, grappa was a working man's drink, made by farmers with the leftover pomace (stems and skins) after wine making. The musty-smelling pile was fermented and then distilled into an extremely strong, highly alcoholic drink that provided much-needed calories during the winter.

By the 1960s the Nonino family, who started out with a portable still that they brought to farms, was producing a high-quality grappa. They had upgraded to a more advanced method in their plant, but their grappa was still made using the winery's leftovers. Enter Giannola, who married Benito Nonino and decided to completely flip the grappa-making process on its head.

Rather than use mixed-up, old leftovers, she had the bold idea to pick up the freshly pressed pomace within hours of its pressing, and distill single varietals using a discontinuous still, which would preserve (she hoped) the aroma of the original grapes. Her husband, Benito, is the mastermind who devised the method, but it was Giannola's vision and passion that resulted in the first single-grape grappa using the Picolit wine grape. Most people thought they were crazy, but once they tasted the brew they were smitten. The Noninos had done what no one had done before: produce a grappa that retained the perfumes and essence of the original grape.

Over the last three decades the revolution that the Noninos started has changed the way the world thinks of grappa. Their stylish bottles are widely imitated, as are their smooth-as-silk grappas and aquavits.

amari

Sharing space in my beloved liquor cabinet is my collection of amari. Like their bitter relatives Campari and Aperol, which are imbibed before a meal, amari are full of herbs and spices that are meant to help that digestive process on its way at the end of the meal. And I have to admit, it's much easier to convince my guests to try some weird and wonderful amari than it is grappa. While grappa is a distilled spirit and has nothing more to soften its bang, amari usually have a "healthy" dose of sugar to soften the edges of those bitter herbs.

The first time I was offered an amaro I wasn't sure I was understanding correctly. It was at the end of a long lunch in Florence. My friend Marietta and I had just worked our way through antipasto, primo, secondo, and dolce. As the waiter finally laid down the bill, along with a complimentary plateful of biscotti, he asked, *"Voi qualcosa per digerere?"* ("Would you like something to help you digest?")

How completely strange, I thought, that this waiter, who had actually been flirting with us both over the course of our three-hour lunch, was now asking if we wanted an Alka-Seltzer, or maybe a laxative? I could understand how he might be concerned after the amount of food and wine Marietta and I had put away, but going so far as to offer a remedy before it was asked for? And while we were still at the table, nibbling on the cookies he had practically forced upon us?

While I gave him a raised eyebrow, Marietta instead responded right away. *"Un Averna per favore."* Since she seemed to know what she was doing, and the waiter was standing there looking at me expectantly, the only thing I could say was *"Anche'io."* ("Me, too.")

The waiter didn't have far to go, turning to a small cart that I really hadn't noticed before. About a dozen bottles contained dark syrupy liquid, which only served to make the brightly colored labels all the more garish. The waiter reached in the back, pulled out a bottle with an old-fashioned yellow label, and poured us each a thimble-size glass.

When Marietta told the waiter she would have an Averna, she was referring to the brand of amaro that she wanted. Like anything else having to do with food and drink in Italy, amari change from region to region, and everyone has their preferred brand. Some are on the sweet side and others are shiver-inducingly bitter. Averna, made in Sicily, is one of the most popular since it's right in the middle between bitter and sweet.

Although all amari look pretty much alike—dark brown to almost black—the flavor profiles couldn't be more different.

This is because they are always made from a mixture of dozens of wild herbs, which change from region to region. There are hundreds of amari produced all over Italy, from Sicily to the Alps, and each has a secretly guarded formula.

when in rome . . . amari and grappa

- Often at the end of a meal the restaurant will offer you an after-dinner drink. Be brave, be bold, and ask for an amaro or grappa and leave the limoncello to the tourists.

- Bring home a bottle. Many amari are never exported, so if you find one you like, buy a bottle to take home. There is usually a surprisingly good selection in most Italian supermarkets.

- Not sure whether to end a meal with a coffee or a shot of grappa? Do both. Have a *caffè coretto* and pour a shot of grappa directly into your coffee.

where to buy amari and grappa in rome

Chirra
Via Torino 132
A place I know almost too well. I usually head here for otherwise difficult-to-find-in-Rome imported bottles of the hard stuff like Maker's Mark when I want an

old-fashioned or something other than supermarket vodka for a martini. But I always end up falling into a trance in front of the huge selection of amari. I just love the names and the designs of Kapriol, Casauria, and Florio. The friendly staff is helpful, and you can actually try some of the amari, since half the shop is a bar.

Angelini Enoteca
Via del Viminale 62

A slightly weirder place. Its dusty windows are stacked with a huge collection of bottles; some empty, some just old and dusty, all interesting. Looking for a bottle of nameless red wine with a label featuring Mussolini or the Pope? This is the place to go. Angelini has been in business since 1880, as the current owner, Enrico, is more than happy to explain. It was his grandfather who opened the shop, when the building was built, and they have been here ever since. Luckily, if you are in the mood for discontinued and hard-to-find regional amari, some of the stock has also been on the shelves for decades. Several dusty bottles of Amaro Kambusa must be among the only left around. They were sitting next to an even dustier bottle of Braulio Riserva (who knew amari even had *riservas*?) Angelini, with their more than 40 amari, seems to cover all the regions—including some that I have a feeling are no longer even part of Italy.

recipes

In my efforts to convert my friends to the ways of grappa, I sneakily rope them in through grappa cocktails. I've created quite a few over the years, making use of both the true grappas (made from the lees of wine) as well as the distillates.

UE Fragolino Cru is one of my favorites to play around with. It is made from the extremely rare Fragolino grape from Friuli, and is a full grape distillate. This may be the most aromatic of all the UEs (grape distillates) with hints of blueberry and wild strawberries.

fragolino cocktail

Serves 1

2 ounces Grappa Cru Fragolino
1 ounce pomegranate juice
1 teaspoon pomegranate molasses
Ice

Place all ingredients in a cocktail shaker with ice, shake until chilled, then pour into a chilled martini glass.

grappa fruit salad

Fresh seasonal fruit
Granulated sugar
Grappa

Make your favorite fresh seasonal fruit salad. It's nice if you have a mix of colors and textures. About an hour before serving, toss with 1 tablespoon of sugar per 2 cups fruit. Add about 2 tablespoons of grappa for each tablespoon of sugar (I used the Carasus, which I happened to have on hand, but you could use Moscato di Nonino Grappa, Grappa Cru Fragolino, or Grappa Cru Picolit). Toss and let sit for an hour.

Note: Storing grappa: After years of thinking I must be drinking grappa in my sleep, I realized that the high alcohol content (from 38 to 45 percent) meant that my precious grappa was evaporating away. Now I always store opened bottles with a small sheet of plastic wrap between the bottle neck and cork.

red currant and grappa cocktail

Serves 1

Most people, when confronted with freshly made fruit juices at the farmers' market, would think "healthy breakfast drink." Me? My mind immediately turns to cocktails.

⅓ cup fresh red currant juice
2 ounces good-quality grappa
1 teaspoon fresh Meyer lemon juice
Ice

Place all the ingredients in a cocktail shaker with ice. Shake until well chilled and strain into a glass.

the eternal city

When I first started my blog in 2009 it was for a very specific reason. My publishers told me that without a "platform" I couldn't hope to reach an audience to sell my book. But the reason that I was writing the blog changed very quickly. Not only did no one want to read a blog that was purely promotional, but also I didn't have any fun writing it—and it showed. So my shift from writing to sell a book to writing about what I'm passionate about—Rome—happened early on. That I chose to focus on food came naturally and was not surprising.

What was surprising, though, was that turning the focus of my blog toward the city where I live, and thought I knew very well, actually changed my point of view. Like anyone else, I not only took my home for granted, but often ignored or just didn't see what was right in front of me. A simple cookie shop in Trastevere, a stop for pizza bianca, and even the bar where I go every day for a midmorning cappuccino became starting points for stories about the city that I love.

When I first began writing my blog I was not intending to become a photographer. Although my career had everything to do with gorgeous photography (I have written six of those big, beautiful coffee-table books about Italy), those images were taken by professional photographers. Even though I was the stylist, producer, and all-around image wrangler,

it was not my eye behind the lens. But in my efforts to make my blog more attractive, I not only became a better photographer, but also began to see beauty in places I never looked before. While I had always loved artichokes, once they were captured in the frame of my lens, I realized how gorgeous they really were. And the diffused light coming through white umbrellas to illuminate a plate of puntarelle, the pastel colors of my favorite gelateria, and the neon sign on my neighborhood bar were things that I could now not only capture, but share.

But when it came time to turn away from my blog and frame my experiences in book form, another thing happened. As I was reading through the more than 700 blog posts I have written over the last five years, and thought about my last four decades in this city, I began to think about time and change. Yes, certainly, I had been changed by the city. But the city itself had both changed and remained exactly the same. It is, as people have called it, "eternal."

While things like more cars, more tourists, and more of just about everything have changed the sleepy city I remember from my days here in the 1970s, I am continuously surprised by just how much has remained the same. The waiter who served me my first taste of carbonara is still bringing my plate to the table when I head back to a favorite restaurant. The same church bells still wake me at seven o'clock each morning. And the same bright green smell of artichokes still almost brings me to tears when I walk into the market on a rainy spring morning.

But change there is, and no more so obvious as when it comes to food. While many of my favorite haunts have closed—butchers, pasta makers, and bakeries—other things have taken their place. A younger generation of Romans is opening new places that, while leaving some traditions behind, are embracing the ingredients and spirit that embodies Rome.

I'm always a bit hesitant to declare my love of change, especially in a city where history is omnipresent. Sometimes I think it is my American way of thinking overriding any sense of being truly Roman that I've by now acquired. Yes, I'm just as in love with the vine-covered walls, shaded restaurant tables, and outdoor markets as the next person. But I also love innovation and the spirit behind the new gourmet panini place around the block, the hipster bar that serves cocktails, or the raw chocolate shop that just opened. I even love the totally unlocal fruit salad that vendors in the market have decided to sell to tourists because it shows a sense of adapting to whatever this city brings.

The other day, when I stopped by my butcher to pick up three pork chops for dinner, we started talking about the changes in our neighborhood of Monti. What started out as a conversation about the vagaries of cell phones (he hates them) turned into a full-blown discussion about progress. Since he was against mobile phones, I expected him to also start in on the new cocktail bar down the street and the fancy organic market around the corner. Instead he declared, "It really bothers me when people start telling me how this neighborhood was better before. I mean, look, when I grew up we were eating bread, water, and sugar for dinner. When I went to take a bath I used a bucket. One day I'd wash my leg, then next my arm. People talk about the charm of going shopping for food every day, buying just what you need from an open market. But you want to know the truth? We bought a ¼ liter of olive oil and 300 grams of spaghetti because that's all we could afford. Sure, Monti was beautiful back then. But it's still beautiful. It's still a neighborhood. It's still our neighborhood. You can't complain about change, you have to embrace it and go forward. Going forward? It's always better than going backward. Every time."

So my blog and this book are works in progress. It's about my Rome, how I came to love it, and how I now share it with others. True, Rome is always changing, but it's been changing for about two thousand years. And it's still here. And, luckily, so am I.

index